As the World Turns… Observations on International Business and Policy, Going International and Transitions

As the World Turns… Observations on International Business and Policy, Going International and Transitions

Michael R. Czinkota

Illustrations by David Clark

CETERUM CENSEO

business**expert**
Press

First published in 2012 by
Business Expert Press, LLC
222 East 46th Street, New York, NY 10017
www.businessexpertpress.com

ISBN-13: 978-1-60649-446-2 (paperback)

ISBN-13: 978-1-60649-447-9 (e-book)

DOI 10.4128/9781606494479

Cover design by Jonathan Pennell and David Clark
Interior design by Exeter Premedia Services Private Ltd.,
Chennai, India

First edition: 2012

10 9 8 7 6 5 4 3 2 1

Printed in the United States of America.

To Ilona and Margaret, who are crucial in carrying the weight

Contents

Foreword

I met Michael Czinkota at the U.S. Department of Commerce during the exciting international trade days of the Reagan Administration. I had just arrived as a former White House Fellow, and he had taken a leave from his professorship at Georgetown University. My contacts at 1600 Pennsylvania Avenue had told me about Michael's sudden appointment. Based on his research, he had written regular commentaries and editorials dealing with international business issues for a variety of newspapers. One of those was the *Chicago Tribune*. At the time, in 1984, there was much congressional action about voluntary import restraints, special tariffs, and restrictions on the import of Japanese cars, so that U.S. manufacturers could recapture market share. Michael had written a column for the *Sunday Tribune* on "Bonuses and Auto Executives" in which he deplored the burden imposed on American consumers through such measures, and called for an end to consumer suffering by focusing on greater automotive industry competitiveness.

President Reagan read a national cross section of editorials and commentaries every weekend. He marked Michael's piece and wrote on the side of it: "Hire him." So, sure enough, the following week Michael received a call at Georgetown, inquiring whether he would be willing to serve in the administration. The position was Deputy Assistant Secretary of Commerce, responsible for Trade Information and Analysis—very fitting for a highly talented researcher and analyst.

I was introduced to him by H. P. Goldfield, then of trade development fame, who achieved major strides in export encouragement, and by Paul Freedenberg, in charge of U.S. export controls, whose job was to restrict strategic trade with adversaries. Even though both of them had quite different policy objectives, when it came to trade, both of them were great fans of Michael and suggested that his thoughts really made a major difference. I thought they were exaggerating, until I became the Director General of the U.S. Foreign and Commercial Service, and benefited constantly from Michael's superb advice. They were right.

During our time in the Reagan Administration—and later on the Bush team, Michael kept on writing his insightful pieces. Of course, now it was not just an academic voicing his analytical perspective, but a government policy maker whose views also necessarily reflected that of the administration. Therefore, his writings needed to be approved by several tiers of officials, in order to ensure that everyone stayed on message. As a result, Michael's freewheeling writings were less positioned to the outside. Rather, his main work consisted of taking important trade policy issues and presenting them in a thoroughly condensed and differentiated fashion, including a brief historical review and possible future developments. He did so brilliantly, in-depth and accompanied by a thorough research of the facts. Of course, it helped that he had already published a leading university text *International Marketing*, and was the Department of Commerce's publisher of the annual *Trade Report* and *Industrial Outlook*, both of them were key analytical products of the U.S. government for a wide international audience.

Thirty years later, Michael Czinkota remains a leading exponent of international business and marketing issues. Returning to Georgetown University in the 1990s, he again writes for a series of internationally oriented publications. On the academic side, he writes for journals, and has been named among the top three most productive international business researchers in the world. His textbook is now in its 10th edition—an outcome achieved only by few academic books and more widely used than ever around the world. Apart from a number of honorary degrees, the School of Global Marketing and Business of the Universidad Ricardo Palma, in Lima, Peru, was recently named after him!

During all this time, Michael has continued to take seriously his desire to analyze, understand, educate, and influence. Since he understands that neither policy makers nor business executives can dedicate much time to reading elaborate manuscripts or books, he takes his research findings and translates them into short, cogent, 750-word pieces. This way, he reaches out directly to key audiences that matter, and precipitates change for a better informed and more successful business world.

Michael Czinkota writes for influential media outlets around the world. For example, he contributes to the *Washington Times* and *Roll Call* in Washington, DC; the *Handelsblatt* and *Frankfurter Allgemeine* in Germany; the *Financial Times* in the United Kingdom; *Le Figaro* in France; *Ovi Magazine* in Finland; and the Shanghai Business Daily, *Japan Today*, *Korea Times*, and *OutlookAfghanistan* in Asia. He has expanded his work through his collaboration with award-winning cartoonist David Clark, who, after back and forth discussions, helps add the 1,000-word equivalent of the picture. He keeps up his great style of blending insight with the occasional dose of humor. Just like medicine does not have to taste bad in order to work, so Michael Czinkota believes that learning and insight do not have to be boring. He reflects his work in and exposure to the business sector, the policy realm, and the heavens of academia. In his broad ranging writings you will feel his ability to blend these quite differ-ent perspectives simultaneously in order to present a holistic context of necessary adjustment and capability. This book will be fun to read, and the production of a smile is no mean feat in light of the limited jocularity of the topics addressed. Even more important, by presenting and pulling together perspectives and their shifts over the past three decades (freely mixed with references to ancient history as well), reading this book will leave you with more understanding, smarter, and more capable to make this world better for all of us.

Happy Reading.

Lew Cramer
Director General, U.S. Foreign and Commercial Service (ret.)
and
President, World Trade Center Utah
Salt Lake City, UT
May 1, 2012

Introduction

Why Read This Book

To paraphrase the philosopher Ludwig von Wittgenstein: "If you are not part of the discussion you are like a boxer who never goes into the ring." It is important to be in the ring, and this book will permit you to be there in the fields of international business and marketing.

We hear a lot about the growth of world trade, globalization, and imbalanced distribution of incomes. Yet, how does one understand all the issues, thoughts, and arguments? How does one develop a time frame and context for these issues? This book helps you to do so.

Over the past 30 years, I have written columns and commentaries for a wide variety of newspapers. In them, I try to provide a long-term perspective of issues, campaigns, and phenomena. Going beyond the flavor of the month and conveying a perspective of historic embeddedness is the key purpose of this book. We can learn from the past, not only by understanding what was done before us, but also by appreciating the context in which changes occur.

The commentary format allows you, the reader, to escape the frequent feeling that learning is unpleasant. Insights from policy makers and firms have taught me that many people do not read academic books or even high-quality journal articles. Working one's way through them is typically considered too laborious and insufficiently stimulating. However, decision makers do read editorials and commentaries, which are less time-consuming to absorb. The opportunity to communicate with leaders is much higher with the short piece. The fact that you are reading these words is offered in evidence. Of course, brevity only concerns the means of delivery. The content should be based on significant research and understanding of an issue. Conciseness combined with insight can lead to understanding and perhaps even cause change.

Over the decades, international business and trade have mushroomed in importance. Social and economic shifts have taken us from the back room discussions of experts to public disputes around the world. From ignorance we have entered the stage of much information. Transparency and accountability offer new directions to businesses and their executives. The emergence of a public moral sense and scrutiny about injustices in an international context increases the pressure on companies and governments to reduce corruption and abandon unsavory practices.

In the 1980s and 1990s, the role of governments shrunk drastically, but is now coming back with a vengeance. After decades of aiming for more open markets, the tendency to restrict imports is rising. In blatant disregard that someone's export has to be someone else's import, governments try to keep their home industries protected and their own economies stable and revitalized, all at the expense of the international competition. As a result, global imbalances persist.

Viewed over the long haul, however, we can distinguish patterns of ebb and flow in the international business and trade arena. Just like Saint Augustine who prayed in about 400 A.D. "Lord, make me chaste, but not yet," policy makers and executives often develop measures that delay or even defeat the easing of international trade and investment flows. But then there are also times where change cannot happen quickly enough, where everyone aims to streamline and fast track legislation and to hasten international accords by limiting the influence of legislative deliberations.

There are the subtle and not so subtle efforts at sanctions and disruptions of trade flows, yet they are often met by opposing interest levels. Repeatedly we see one side, which is losing contracts, blaming it all on the corruption and nepotism on part of the winners. Yet, culturally, the closeness to family and desire to help one's own environment in a home country context, can be an obligation rather than a deviation. Laws can be seen both as rigorous structural supports for economic development, or as substantial barriers to growth.

The use and meaning of terminology also has (often temporary) major effects. For example, for decades, the use of the term *most favored nation* (MFN) has led to demonstrations and even street battles by those who did not want to favor a particular country. Now, the problem has gone away, since governments have changed the terminology and only speak of *normal trade relations* (NTR), a goal that seems to be acceptable to all. Definitions that shape our understanding of core issues such as *fairness, market gaps*, *dumping*, and *natural*, can be changed or amended, and thus presented within a new reality. Nowadays, one discusses and begins to reevaluate the meaning and adjustment of key business pillars such as risk, competition, profit, and ownership, which perhaps gradually prepares us for a new environment. Many of today's business executives discover that their activities are but one integral component of society. Politics, security, and religion are only some of the other dimensions that can be held in higher esteem than economics and business by society. Those who structure their arguments based on business principles alone may eventually find themselves on the losing side.

Futurity in general is, in many ways, not all that innovative, but reflective of ongoing and even repetitive change. Just consider how different things will be in a mere 50 years—keeping in mind that the ballpoint pen only came to the U.S. market in 1945, the computer game Pong only became available in 1972, and electronic or e-mail on personal computers only advanced in the late 1980s. Will we appear as retro to our descendants as our ancestors appear to us today (if we bother to look)? Yet, we always are only a brief constant in a world of change.

We discuss the new phenomenon of pirates in Somalia—though the profession was riding high in the Caribbean or during Roman times in Sicily. We highlight the disruptions from terrorism but neglect that already the crusaders wrote home about their fear of terror. We debate new approaches to teaching and communication, but don't stop to think what effect Gutenberg's printing press, wireless telegraphy, or the introduction of radio had on business and society. We deplore the differentiation of groups based on religion, but conveniently forget the impact of Torquemada and the inquisition, the consequences of Luther's theses on the church doors of Wittenberg, the persecution of Jews, or the discrimination against Mormons.

Each article and the accompanying cartoon (remember, a picture can be worth a thousand words) represent a thought opportunity to chew on. The reading will take only a short time; your major investment will be made in the chewing. I hope that the opportunity for comparisons, the recognition of the presence both of rapid shifts but also of permanence, and the appreciation that in many instances the future was 2000 years ago, provides for good thought stimuli. Be it for bedtime reading, for beefing up on a topic before a "wise table dinner," or just for racking the brain, I wish you well with these pages. If you wish to expand your exposure to my thinking, there is an earlier book of mine, titled *As I Was Saying*, with a focus on observations in international business and trade policy, exports, education, and the future.

Some people believe that "if it's not on Google, it does not exist." Others proclaim that all the newfangled activities are too overpowering and irrelevant. Here is good news for both camps: Many of my contributions were published in pre-Google days, which, hopefully, helps with their gravitas. Many articles were also picked up by media search engines and are downloaded regularly—so we are not losing relevance. Overall, keep in mind that life tends to be hectic and short. Often, we no longer huddle around the fireplace to read and contemplate. This book represents an effort to revive such an old custom. Enjoy the read!

In completing this work, I thank the members of my research team, in particular Ireene Leoncio, Sophia Berhie, and Elizabeth Garbitelli; all of Georgetown University. Gratitude is also due to my Georgetown colleagues, Professor Ronkainen, Professor Cooke, and Professor Skuba. Their insights and debates keep international business alive at Georgetown's McDonough School of Business. I also am thankful to the economic kindness of the editors and newspapers who have given me permission to reprint my articles. Heartfelt thanks to David Clark, the award-winning artist who has provided the visual stimuli for this book and my annual calendar. Most of all, I am grateful to my wife Ilona Czinkota who is a major arbiter for the quality of my writings. Early or late in the day, she is willing to provide suggestions. My daughter Margaret comments as well, with much enthusiasm and interest. Both mother and daughter are great sounding boards and come up with excellent questions and solutions. Thanks to all of you!

Michael R. Czinkota
Washington, DC
May 6, 2012

On International Business
and Policy

U.S. Election and International Business

Tuesday's U.S. election will determine the political landscape for the next two years. But though we know that all politics are local, globalization provides all these local politics with major influence on the international marketplace.

Though there is no strict cohesion within Democrats, the Republicans, and the Tea Party, an examination of their typical perspectives on international business issues may be helpful.

Support payments for the agricultural sector, infant industries, and worker adjustment assistance will be favored by Democrats, opposed by Republicans, and viewed with dismay by Tea Party players.

Originally published in the *Korea Times*, November 1, 2010. Used with permission of Michael R. Czinkota and the *Korea Times*.

Tax abatements to encourage domestic investment, tax deferrals for foreign profits, and reduced taxation of income earned abroad will be opposed by Democrats, thus raising taxes on foreign activities.

Republicans favor increased deferrals. Tea Party members are opposed to more government involvement in general, but might find good reason to support locals.

Protection against imports is more likely to be supported by Democrats. Past actions provided large benefits to few firms, and the costs were borne by many. Now there will be smaller benefits to many by taking aggressively from a few.

Exchange rate regimes are crucial. Trade used to drive currency values, but now exchange rates dominate trade. All three groups see exchange rate issues as important.

For Democrats this is another tool for international negotiations. Republicans tend to rely more on market forces—but have demonstrated their willingness to help these forces along. Tea Party players are most likely to stay away from interference in floating exchange rates.

For international institutions, such as the World Bank, the International Monetary Fund (IMF), and the World Trade Organization (WTO), Democrats tend to demand a broadening of activities, with no new funds.

Republicans will invest in rearguard actions to preserve U.S. preeminence and may even provide some creative funding in support of such a goal.

In foreign policy, Democrats are more likely to seek negotiated political solutions. In contrast, Republicans and Tea Party players recognize opportunities for a nexus between trade policy and foreign policy to bridge relational gaps.

There is also a growing indifference, if not disdain of international business concerns by voters.

The Wall Street Journal reports that the American public is increasingly hostile to free trade. Eighty-four percent of Democrats and 90% of Republicans are fearful of outsourcing. Congress will find it quite difficult to exercise leadership if there are no followers.

Non-voters not interested or disenchanted require major new reasons to get involved and may become motivated by charisma or focused bitterness. Already chomping at the bit are the teenagers who are old enough to understand how their future is being mortgaged but too young to vote.

They sense frustration, disappointment, and anger. There will be a payback for the "domestics" who screwed it all up, says my daughter Margaret!

So what needs to be done? An unskilled and unmotivated worker in the U.S. cannot compete with a similar Chinese or Indian laborer. Education and interest will be for many the determining lifestyle factor.

At the same time, not everybody needs to go to college. Plumbing or landscaping are activities of dignity, necessity, and virtue, and deserve to be skillfully taught and learned, rather than looked down upon.

In an age of participation, people no longer just trade their work for money. Firms need to provide context for activities and their repercussions.

Everyone in the U.S. knows about the trauma of international competition, but few are aware of its prosperity. Job reductions are familiar, while new jobs are obscure. Firms must let the world know about growth and profits.

Instead of TV shows on how to get rich by picking random brief cases, it is high time to launch a show on New York exporters or to launch a national competition on how to resolve international business obstacles.

After the election, we can expect more introspection overall on part of the United States. Export issues will gain support, with much less enthusiasm about imports.

There will be limited encouragement of inward investments. Trade treaties, once modified for U.S. benefit are likely to be ratified. Ongoing difficulties precipitated by large budget deficits, will encourage finding a foreign scapegoats.

President Obama, in keeping with established tradition, will increase his international travel and exposure, which will translate into very limited financial support by Congress.

Overall, in terms of public enthusiasm, international trade and investment issues are likely to go back to the conditions of the early 1980s. Relevant for specialists, but held at bay by a key focus on domestic concerns.

The Punishment of Banks: to Whose Benefit?

Large banks are under siege by governments. There are widespread cries of outrage as banks announce their bonuses for 2009 performance. In the UK, Alistair Darling, the finance minister, already revealed a 50% "super-tax" on all UK bank bonuses above £25,000 (about $40,000). France has announced that it will enact a similar tax.

In the U.S., President Barack Obama has announced the imposition of a fee on large finance firms to "recoup" public funds spent in the Troubled Asset Relief Program, irrespective of whether the banks wanted

With C. Skuba. Originally published in the *Japan Today*, February 3, 2010. Used with permission of Michael R. Czinkota and the *Japan Today*.

to participate or not. There is talk of breaking up large banks in order to avoid ever again the problem of institutions that are too large to fail.

Two key economic concepts are under attack by governments. First is the principle of comparative advantage. Ironically, in light of British government's action, the term was popularized almost 200 years ago by Briton David Ricardo. There seems to be a great willingness to do away with the value of this advantage overnight. It took decades, despite significant competition from other financial centers such as Frankfurt and Singapore, for London to develop financial operations superior to others.

That leads to the second concept under attack—clustering. Since birds of a feather flock together, good performers have been attracted to a few locations of financial excellence. The existence of a comparative advantage of the financial sector attracted related and supporting industries as well. London and New York therefore became key markets, attracting key players who were paid top rewards. Quite a perpetuum mobile if not disturbed!

However, disturbances did occur, as was evident in the last two years. Markets were not as successful as one would like them to be. There were large losses due to opaqueness in corporate activities and high-risk exposure. Are we now seeking to find ways to reform finance in order to offer more transparency and better risk management?

Apparently not. The UK government seems to believe that curtailing the work of markets will improve conditions. Even conservative-led governments in France and Germany are leveraging public opinion to increasingly tax the banks. When public anger is high, it can easily be used to support political action.

Taxation is an easy recourse, but is it the right course? Finance employees are angered by any "supertax." Many view the action as unfair and pandering to short-term populism. In a business where individuals can generate millions of pounds worth of profits (and losses), a trigger amount of £25,000 seems very low. Critics also fear that special taxes and fees would damage the attractiveness of any current financial center.

In a global environment, one can expect bankers and banks to look at alternatives such as Hong Kong, Singapore, or Geneva. Some governments might well see new opportunities to attract financial businesses and shift comparative advantage. Perhaps Silvio Berlusconi, with visions of renewed Medici splendor, might offer Milan as the bank-friendly city? Could Chancellor Angela Merkel of Germany may reposition Frankfurt as the new Mecca for financiers? Is this the time to see Shanghai emerge as the global super banking center?

So far, governments reject any criticisms of their special assessments as humbug. They justify the "one-off" tax with the argument that banks were able to realize profits, and subsequently pay large bonuses, in large part due to the government's "bail-out" of the banking system. While there is merit to this argument, we advise a more prudent approach supportive of a renewed and thriving financial system and limited in its imposition of pain on high performing-financial executives. We should not punish excellence.

There have been corporate compensation structures that rewarded top executives at levels beyond their contributions to the firm. Reform is needed. While a forceful counterpunch against an industry and its employees may lead to short-term popular contentment, one should bear in mind that in the long run, there is little support for high levels of taxation. As we pursue needed reforms, let's not put a desire for retribution over good business sense.

Government actions can have significant indirect effects. We are reminded of the Empress dowager Tz'u-hsi. In 1896, in order to finance the renovation of the summer palace, she impounded funds that had been designated for Chinese shipping and its navy. As a result, China's participation in world trade virtually ground to a halt. In the subsequent decades, China operated almost in total isolation, without any transfer of knowledge from the outside, without major inflow of goods, and without the innovation and productivity increases that result from international exposure.

A few locations have laboriously built comparative advantage for their financial sector. Prosperous financial firms provide treasure and opportunity to the fortunate societies in which they cluster. Given today's mobility of both industries and employees, banks that are convinced of their righteousness, can fight back and move core units to business friendly locations.

Businesses, in general, need to remember that they are but one integral component of society. The level and structure of their profits and executive compensation should reflect a firm's long term best interests within an overall societal context. MBA programs without an emphasis on such context and proportionality, must revise such shortcomings in their teaching. Legislators and government in turn need to recognize the direct and indirect effects of their actions on global conditions. While reforms are good and necessary, the breaking up of a comparative advantage and successful clusters without a productive replacement is a risky strategy.

The End of Corruption?

I recently attended a breakfast meeting with U.S. Secretary of Commerce Gary Locke and Angel Gurria, Secretary General of the Organization for Economic Co-operation and Development. The meeting was sponsored by Transparency International and focused on the need to continue reducing global corruption.

Several Thoughts Stand Out

Globally, corruption is estimated to comprise between 5% and 20% of contract amounts. There are two major kinds of payments in the corruption

Originally published in the *Japan Today*, December 20, 2009. Used with permission of Michael R. Czinkota and the *Japan Today*.

context: One consists of paying a foreign government (or an official) to do something they should not be doing (letting a contract on special terms). The second is to pay someone to do something they are supposed to do (facilitating payments). It's the first type of payment that really matters in terms of distortion of markets and economic benefits.

This is not a victimless crime. Such corruption causes reduction of competition, lessening of quality, increases in prices, and the deprivation of those who lose out on goods, services or funding. Poor countries suffer the most from bribery schemes, because their citizens and companies have few, if any, alternatives. That is what makes rules against corruption so important. They help equalize the playing field and lets all capable players participate.

There remains much work to be done, but over the last 10 years the extent of corruption has been reduced on a global level. The United States looked unrealistic, and perhaps even eccentric when the U.S. Congress passed the Foreign Corrupt Practices Act (FCPA) in 1977, making it illegal for publicly held companies to bribe foreign officials. Many U.S. firms complained about this law, arguing that in many countries the payment of bribes was commonplace and tax deductible. They also claimed that the law hindered their efforts to compete internationally against companies from countries that had no such anti-bribery laws. Research at the time supported this claim by indicating that in the years after the anti-bribery legislation was enacted, U.S. business activity declined precipitously in those countries in which government officials routinely received bribes.

Since then, the issue of bribery has taken on new momentum. Thirty-eight countries are now subscribing to the OECD rules (eight more than its membership of 30 nations) which prohibit the bribery of public officials. Among them are South Korea, Japan, Mexico, South Africa, and Argentina. Large companies, such as Siemens, have been taken to court and punished for paying bribes. Increasingly, companies state that the anti-bribery drive now gives them a clear rationale to say "no" when bribes are demanded.

The progress is good. Several questions remain though: Should rules across borders be the same, particularly when it comes to the allocation of expenses and the treatment of family members, or should there be an acknowledged role for cultural differences? What is a realistic level of how low we can expect to drive this pernicious waste. Should we develop a time table to drive down corruption even further—either in absolute figures (down from the annual $1 trillion that Transparency International estimates) or down to, say, less than 3% of contract value?

What should the punishment be for those who continue to engage in bribery? Should one just drive the companies and politicians who violate the public trust out of business? Wouldn't such steps be unfair to most of the employees of these firms who had no inkling of illegal activities? Should there be a statute of limitations for prosecution or should firms and individuals be forever exposed to the consequences of wrongful behavior in the past? Who should be given any disgorgement of ill-gotten proceeds: The party whose money was misappropriated or the one that did not receive the benefits to which it was entitled?

The American Taxpayer's Global Investment

As the new General Motors "gets down to business," its current owners are grappling with the preservation of the company and a portion of its jobs. Over time, they will also focus on what it will take to get a good return. The American taxpayer, in the form of the U.S. government, now owns 60 percent of a piece of America's business heritage and way of life. GM is promising "reinvention" and "the rebirth of the American car." As a part of that reinvention, GM must become a key global competitor who cannot only sell against foreign competition in the United States, but will also succeed abroad.

GM cannot succeed solely as an American car company. Its industry is among the most competitive in the world. For any firm to prosper, global

With C. Skuba. Originally published in the *Roll Call*, June 8, 2009. Used with permission of Michael R. Czinkota and the *Roll Call*.

sales and operations efficiencies are a *sine qua non*. Of course, the new GM already has an international component in its ownership structure with a 12.5 percent stake from the governments of Canada and Ontario. The U.S. and Canadian auto industries are intricately interconnected with some vehicles crossing the border, an average of seven times over the course of production. That said, GM's future lies outside of North America.

Ninety-five percent of the world's customers live outside the United States. Significantly more cars will be sold this year in both Europe and Asia than in the U.S. Car purchases in China, India, and Brazil through April exceed U.S. volume when annualized. What's more, GM is doing very well in both China and Brazil. China is the company's largest growth market. *China Daily* reports that GM has announced the target of doubling sales in China over the next five years and opening a new factory there to meet increased demand. Americans should see that as good news.

Shifting global demand requires adjustments in production capacity and product. Consistent with the product cycle theory, over time, established products are produced in new locations with more local advantages. New production sites with lower cost structures keep supplying the global market. Unless a company expands internationally, these production sites will belong to competitors. For GM, a goal to become equals with the competition is not good enough. GM must excel again.

Shifts to new plants and new countries will be difficult for Americans to swallow as GM, in spite of huge U.S. government subsidies, closes factories and eliminates jobs at home. The issue will become particularly sensitive when GM uses overseas production facilities to import cars to the United States. Yet, to perform in its post-bankruptcy life, GM will need to rationalize its global production platform to maximize economies of scale and eliminate waste. Inefficient production is one of the principal reasons for GM's Chapter 11 filing and should not be championed in the guise of protecting American jobs.

GM has an uphill battle in the United States. The firm currently has about 20% of the highly segmented U.S. auto market. Americans may love "baseball, hot dogs, apple pie and Chevrolet," but they also love their Toyotas and Volkswagens and Kias. Consumers are looking for cars that meet their individual needs, and they have many alternatives. GM will need great products and marketing just to regain more share of the home market.

Even more critically, GM must compete globally or be marginalized as a niche competitor. GM's reinvention right now is the divestiture of some of its key operations abroad, particularly Opel in Europe. By ceding Europe to the competition, GM will certainly be leaner, but it also loses a significant presence in a very important global auto market. Can GM's eventual recovery come in the form of cars designed only for greener U.S. consumers? We don't think so. If the firm is to compete again with superb products in the U.S. market, then these very same products will and must compete abroad. Otherwise, ongoing protective government measures will only keep inefficiencies alive.

The Obama administration may not intend to be an active manager of the new GM, but its policies on trade, foreign investment, and taxation shape the company's future. The taxpayer as investor should insist on the new GM producing the kind of quality products that future global consumers need and want. The search for additional investors from abroad must also continue. At the same time, government policies must allow and even encourage GM to be competitive not just at home, but also abroad. While they may not have bargained for it, U.S. taxpayers are now invested in global competition.

Presidential Candidate's Overseas Travel

Barack Obama, a key candidate and the presumptive nominee for the U.S. presidency, is traveling around the globe. Some claim it to be a bit unusual for a non-elected candidate to undertake such a trip. But such visits should be welcomed—they are great opportunities for listening and learning. Both candidates should consider regular outreach to the world. If physical travel is not possible, there should at least be virtual contact.

Current outreach differs in major ways from earlier trips by U.S. leaders. For many decades, U.S. leaders toured nations to impart their views, while bearing policy gifts to the countries visited.

Originally published in the *Korea Times*, July 27, 2008. Used with permission of Michael R. Czinkota and the *Korea Times*.

The goal was for others to better understand what the United States stood for, and what new policy initiatives meant. When international statesmen came to visit the United States, they typically expected to be briefed on new U.S. positions, demonstrate their closeness with U.S. policymakers, and receive special concessions.

In the present economic and political climate, the tables are turned. Now U.S. leaders need to learn and listen in order to integrate global perspectives into their thinking. Their acceptance abroad will influence the U.S. view of a candidate's capability.

Hosts no longer need to rely on intermediaries and be misled in outcome expectations, as was the case in the last U.S. elections. Instead of receiving gifts, they need to consider what policy concessions and support they can offer to the United States.

The world is looking forward to the next U.S. administration. New directions are expected on military, economic, and political issues. After eight years, the entrenched policies and approaches of any administration will restrain flexibility. It is as though the ship of state has become weighed down by the many crustaceans attached to its keel. The dislodging of the barnacles may improve its speed and maneuverability.

Now that there is an early opportunity for the addressing of new directions, it is important to consider what world leaders could be prepared to present to their visitors in support of a redefined partnership. Here are some possible offerings:

Canada and Mexico—the U.S.' largest and closest partners, could provide close collaboration in the energy field.

Mexico's offer could focus on developing its internal market, in order to reduce the emigration pressures on its citizens. Together with other Central and South American partners, it could volunteer increased efforts, aimed at restricting drug production and trafficking.

Europe, an economic superpower, could acknowledge that politics do play a role in economic issues. Of concern are interest rates, the strength of the dollar and energy prices. A greater openness to genetically modified organisms (GMOs) would improve agricultural policies and negotiations.

Stronger enforcement of anti-bribery rules could relieve a major burden for the United States. There can be much more civilian assistance and financial contribution by the EU in both Afghanistan and Iraq, and more collaboration on Iran.

Greater European investment in Africa, specifically by France and Italy, could demonstrate European commitment to hotspots, such as Sudan, Zimbabwe, and Kenya.

Given global concerns about energy, a new proposal could create a Global Energy Conservation Corps. Building on discussions held in Liechtenstein, young people could spend time learning about the tools, devices, and measurement of energy conservation and then reach out globally.

A hands-on commitment to service and sustainability would increase emotional connections and networking on a global scale.

Asia could offer more defense and more food to the world. Quotas, duties, and export bans of foodstuffs could be voluntarily reduced.

Vietnam, India, Cambodia, and Japan could divest their stockpiles to increase supply. Others could lead by supporting openness, freedom, and individual liberty and demonstrate to the world that there is a common vision of a human future.

A jumpstart of the Doha Round of trade negotiations could reconfirm global support for trade and investment flows. Currently, only the fierce opposition of those who suffer from globalization is visible.

Vitriolic anti-globalization campaigns are generated, even if only a small portion of troubles emanate from international issues. Initiatives and collaboration from those who gain from international economic activity are crucial. Success needs much greater visibility and continuity, to discourage those worshipping on the altar of protectionism.

African leaders need to prevent cultural conflicts from becoming irreconcilable. They must ensure that societies are cohesive, linked, and ready for collaboration. Joint enforcement of behavioral standards for human dignity would be essential.

Islamic leadership could demonstrate its willingness to be more inclusive and offer an increased commitment to the reduction of discrimination against non-Muslims. Such collaboration should clarify that there is no orchestrated international effort against Islam.

The Bush administration intended to leverage U.S. humility in foreign policy. However, unforeseen events derailed this plan. Getting to know each other more is good, as is ongoing communication.

Right now, there is a need for clear, supportive, and specific actions, which key nations can propose to the U.S., in order to reaffirm a more equitable international partnership. Candidates around the globe should travel more to increase their exposure and understanding.

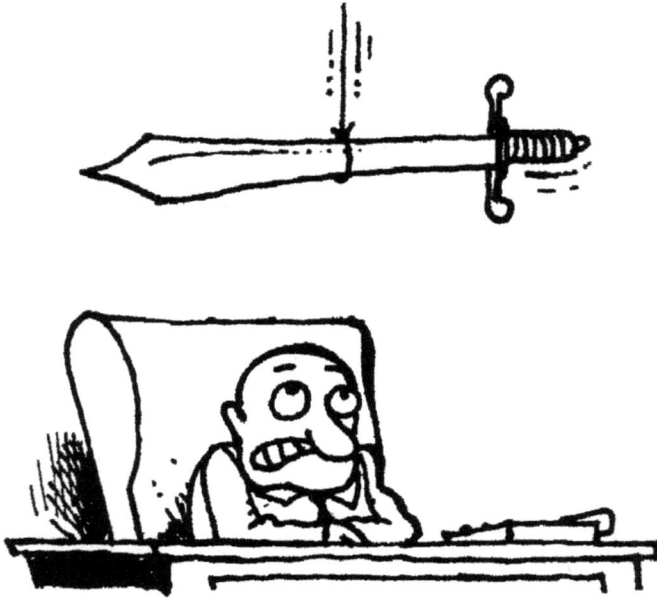

MFN's Riskier Renewal Rite

The debate about renewing most favored nation (MFN) status for Chinese imports into the United States, provides a sense of déjà vu. This annual ritual demands major policy concessions from China; some progress will be achieved; come June we'll all be back to business as usual. Let this be a wake-up call! Things are different this time around. There really will be a non-renewal of MFN unless those who want and need trade with China start fighting hard. Now.

Originally published in *The Washington Times*, May 8, 1994. Used with permission of Michael R. Czinkota and *The Washington Times*.

Traditionally, three perspectives have existed regarding MFN and China. The very conservative one opposes extending such benefits to communists. The very liberal one opposes them on grounds of human rights violations. In the middle of both is the traditional support for MFN on grounds of overwhelming business interests. So far, the Boeing argument has always won out.

But this administration has a dire need and the capability to say no to MFN. The election was won based on the promise of change, a new covenant, a new attitude, and a new orientation. But with healthcare stalled, the crime bill in limbo, and the job corps decimated, there are very few concrete results to point to, apart from the tax increase. An MFN suspension cannot only demonstrate a new direction, but can also replace those pesky Whitewater headlines. Furthermore, since the tough approach seems to work at least somewhat with Japan, why not try it with China?

More importantly, this administration has managed to "Boeing-proof" itself. With the February announcement of the $6 billion sale of airplanes to Saudi Arabia and the telecommunication deal to be announced by month's end, this administration has already bestowed major benefits on two major U.S. export industries who would suffer the most from a MFN nonrenewal. These benefits and the promise of more government-obtained contracts from abroad will help ease the burden of any unfavorable administration action. Finally, last fall's bruising debate over the North American Free Trade Agreement generated much ill will with the unions. What better way to share the pain than to dramatically reduce imports of low-wage goods? With superb skill, this administration has been able to orchestrate a new framework in which a denial of MFN makes for excellent politics. Unfortunately, doing so is still bad policy.

First, a clarifying remark on the meaning of the term "most favored nation." Contrary to frequent perception, MFN does not imply any favorable treatment for a country's exports. Rather, MFN means that, in accordance with international trading rules, a country's exports are not treated any worse than the exports of other nations. MFN is the equal opportunity clause of the grading community that only the United States considers a privilege rather than a right.

The effects of not renewing MFN are major. U.S. prices of products customarily sourced from China, such as textiles and shoes, will temporarily skyrocket until new suppliers can be found and production can be shifted. U.S. firms will be excluded from the Chinese market, one of the key areas of world market growth, and the fertile field will be left to competitors. Some believe that China would not retaliate against U.S. investors because that would be to the disadvantage of the Chinese economy. But, if we are not beyond shooting ourselves in the foot, maybe the Chinese aren't either. And even if the Chinese government does nothing directly against U.S. investors in China, many of them will be hurt by their heavy dependence on imports from the United States. For example, Continental Grain will not be able to produce much feedstock in China without critical imports from back home. Most importantly, however, just as the memories of the Carter grain embargo begin to fade, U.S. firms will again revive their reputation for unreliability. Nonrenewal of MFN will be a major blow to our global business success, just when we need an increased economic world presence to make up for our military withdrawals.

Our firms must recognize that this time, the danger to MFN is real. The stars are unfavorable. It is imperative to take action now to avert such a disaster. Our corporations must let the administration know now about the effects of MFN curtailment. The number of jobs at stake, the long-term risks to competitiveness, and the ceding of hard-fought business territory to the competition cannot be permitted. For the sake of human rights, MFN must be renewed. After all, it will be a growing standard of living together with a growing middle class that will bring about permanent change for the better in China.

Effects of September 11 on Marketing Policy

The terror of September 11 is a key fissure in American lives. At George-town's McDonough School of Business, we investigated the repercussions of the terror on international marketing policy and corporate practices. We found a new era of common sense characterized by five key dimensions.

The first is a common sense of vulnerability. What happened in New York and Washington, D.C., can occur in any location around the globe.

There is a common sense of outrage—no moral ambivalence here. These attacks touch individuals like a cold wind that makes sweat-beaded skin shiver.

Originally published in *The Japan Times*, January 15, 2002. Used with permission of Michael R. Czinkota and *The Japan Times*.

There is a renewed global common sense of collaboration. The past decade has seen a reluctance of nations to support joint direction, which has led to international policy stalemates. Today, a new understanding of a common future requires us to rely on each other.

There are new politics of common sense, best seen by the new round of trade talks. Important concessions were required from everyone in Doha, but September 11 helped to place highly controversial issues—such as agricultural subsidies, dumping regulations, property rights, and investment rules—on the table. Although trade negotiations will not be easy, the road toward progress has been opened.

There is a new sense of what we have in common. For too long, global discussions were dominated by all the things that make us different. Now there is more thinking of those issues that bring us together.

On the corporate side, we found important changes in the areas of customer management, people management, production management, and logistics.

Managers now consider the development of customer trade portfolios more carefully. Dependence on any region or customer are limited to reduce a firm's exposure in case of conflict; systematic market development can then balance existing exposure.

Corporations have become more sensitive to the possibility of misuse of their exports. There is more intensive scrutiny of orders received, of customers, and of product use before an order is shipped.

Heightened scrutiny also extends to employees. Firms take a closer look at credentials and claims. The issue of culture and diversity has taken on greater importance. Managers who had previously only focused on the bottom line now develop a greater appreciation for differences among employees. As one executive put it, "We look at each other much more closely and that makes you understand things better."

Members of the supply chain want to identify and manage their dependence on international inputs. Industrial customers are often seen as pushing for U.S.-based sourcing to avoid interruptions. Customers feel better when their goods are produced in West Virginia or Kentucky than when their shipments come from Argentina or Greece.

Companies have accepted that the international pipeline has slowed down. Firms with international just-in-time delivery systems are still being affected months later due to increased security measures. Some are thinking about replacing international shipments with domestic ones, where local trucking would replace transborder movement and eliminate the use of vulnerable ports. Hub-and-spoke distributors now discover how transshipments add to time delays. Plans for fewer hubs and more direct connections may lead to higher prices but more consistent shipments within a shorter time.

September 11 is a shared experience that has strengthened U.S. resolve, affirmed U.S. global leadership, and opened new strategic dimensions in policy, a recent *Washington Post* and corporate thinking. There is an increased desire for collaboration. Higher efficiency and success are likely if the United States and its firms further refine their ability to form partnerships. International networks will become much more pronounced. Becoming part of them will be a key challenge for the international marketer.

There is a greater need for trust as a key component of an international marketing relationship, both on the customer and the supplier side. The ability to engender such trust may well become decisive to international marketing success. Firms are more willing to make a commitment to their partners, which imply a longer-term time frame and allows for a thrust to continue even after the glue of its initial impetus has become brittle.

A recent *Washington Post* survey reports that most respondents feel that the attacks have permanently changed U.S. for the better. In the international marketing field, we clearly see a new willingness to stand together, to join forces, face down adversity, and persist in one's goals. Standing together improves America's outlook on the future and also offers global progress toward a better quality of life.

Don't Kill the Commerce Department

Proposing the dissolution of a government agency is like breaking off a bad relationship: The notion of ending it may seem like a bold and welcome idea.

But there is nothing bold or even unique about proposing the dismemberment of the Commerce Department, as Republican budget cutters have done. It has been done before.

In 1913, the labor section was removed to form the Department of Labor. In 1966, the transportation office became the Department of Transportation. Other offices became the Federal Trade Commission and

---

Originally published in the *Journal of Commerce*, June 7, 1995: 8A. Used with permission of Michael R. Czinkota and the *Journal of Commerce*.

the Federal Aviation Administration. The growth of these "appendages" conjures up an image of a modern-day Hydra: Whenever one head is cut off, it is replaced by two new ones.

Perhaps this is the time for another Herculean effort. Yet before rushing into battle, let's consider some facts. The Commerce Department is quite large—36,000 employees—but it has many duties. Indeed, there are important reasons for most of the department's operations. When the U.S. Trade Representative announces trade sanctions, it is the Commerce Department staff that does the research on products to target. When intellectual property rights are debated, it is the Commerce that has registered the patents. When weather reports appear in newspapers or on television, it is the Commerce that provided the data. These functions are vital and, in many instances, cannot or will not be taken on by the private sector.

Take for example the International Trade Administration: With its analytical and promotional work, this group delivers an increase in exports and jobs.

Detractors argue that these activities are either not valuable, since they only shift resources between firms, or that the private sector can do them just as well or better. Here is the reality: Take a firm that operates only domestically. It has gradually learned about its market, customers, and products and, with growing experience, has managed to decrease its risk. When this firm goes international, it encounters volatile currencies, greater distances, new forms of transportation, and changes in government regulations, legal systems, languages, cultural diversity, and demand patterns.

Due to a lack of knowledge about the new environment, management's perception of risk exposure grows. At the same time, the investment needs of the international effort cause the immediate product expectations to deteriorate. This leads, in the short term, to a situation of rising risk and decreasing profitability.

Although there is substantial evidence that in the longer run international profit levels will rise above the ones achieved domestically, the short-term experience leads to a lack of export commitment.

Export assistance is crucial in helping firms over this rough patch. The Commercial Service provides such help by opening doors, furnishing information, evaluating clients, and locating partners. It uses the government's economies of scale to lower the risk or increase the profitability of firms. And all this occurs with the hard work of relatively few individuals and with a smaller export promotion budget than say, France or Canada.

One could wait for the private sector to take on these functions. There are, after all, freight forwarders, trading companies, and consultants. But their incremental profit from such assistance is too small and the worldwide task too large for them to jump into action.

Using a lighthouse analogy, if ships run aground on hidden reefs, there may well be an incentives for a company to build a lighthouse. But it may take a long time and many lost ships to make it happen.

It makes sense to periodically scrutinize Commerce's operations. Some congressional mandates for extraneous activities should be removed. In times of shifting technologies, booming tourism, and declining export controls, surely some offices can shrink or merge. Newly structured user fees should be investigated. More measures of effectiveness should be introduced to evaluate the return on investment for taxpayer money and to provide guidance for program reduction or expansion. And yes, the Commerce Department Aquarium should go. But the Department of Commerce should continue to do what it does well—work on behalf of industry, gather data, and support government operations. Let's not throw out vital functions with the fish!

On Going International

Why International Marketing?

Five Core Benefits Explain Key Rationale

For many years I've worked in the international marketing field. I know about the field's importance and its relevance to people and firms. In my work with executives, I regularly challenge them to review their most basic assumptions. Just as daily exposure to our children prevents us from gauging how grown-up they have become, mangers might not notice how international marketing has changed because of shifts in society by

Originally published in the *AMA Marketing Management*, July 6, 2011. Used with permission of Michael R. Czinkota and the *AMA Marketing Management*.

individuals or the general environment. We have to devote thought and inquiry to identify what these changes are and the measures we need to take in order to successfully cope with them. I regularly conduct my own assessment of the shifts in my field of international marketing so that I can recalibrate my knowledge and activities.

In the past years there have been major adjustments relevant to international marketing. For example, when domestic economic activities are down, international marketing dips even more dramatically. Austerity brings global changes in production and consumption patterns and introduces new dimensions in the decision-making process. The role of governments is growing by leaps and bounds, making them key entities to dictate the direction and strength of international marketing activities. There is a rising tendency to restrict imports and encourage exports, in order to keep home industries safe and gradually reduce global imbalances. People also are changing their views of the international arena, particularly in a time when terrorism imposes daily reminders on us.

My research on the extent of awareness of, interest in, and dedication to internationalization in the United States indicates a decrease in the extent of international orientation. This shift is unfortunate, but understandable. One way I measure internationalization is the corporate name registrations with the U.S. Securities and Exchange Commission. In the United States, all publicly held companies have to register with the SEC, but there is a great deal of flexibility as to the new name one can choose. In looking at the names registered during the 1990s until 2001, there used to be a strong tendency to select a name that had some international connotation. Consider the French baguette company, the Asian restaurant chain, and the global charity. Sometimes the use of the "international" label does not even reflect any corporate activity abroad, but rather is just considered to be cool to customers. But according to the SEC, international dimensions dropped after 2002 by more than 30 percent while domestic and local affiliations rapidly rose. Now we are looking at the West Coast clothing enterprise and the New York shipping company. With growing globalization there is also more information and perhaps less romanticism about international issues. For example, no longer can the budding international marketer expect to be only active on the "Elizabeth Arden" circuit of London, Paris, and Rome. Nowadays, the route is much more likely to encompass Ingolstadt, Iguazu and Incheon.

In order to refresh my "in the trenches" perspective, I queried international executives to gauge their views on international marketing. The key issues I asked them to address were the benefits, joys, fears, drawbacks, and challenges of international marketing. This column covers the five core benefits revealed, including a brief reflection of the key rationale for their high impact perception.

Freedom

International marketing is a notion of freedom. Growing up in the Soviet Union there simply was no freedom of choice. I could never dream of studying abroad or working for an American company. I like having the choice and the freedom to choose for myself. It removes boundaries between nations and grants more opportunities to gain better skills and exposure to different cultures.

Opportunity and Contentment

International marketing is the best way to raise national power and status for nations with limited resources and territory. It is a key factor that strengthens both nations and individuals. International marketing is the inspiration of life. It is an efficient way of doing business globally and it tends to highlight any administration that succumbs to corruption. The aim of international marketing is to unite the world with a better era for the human race as competitive cooperation supersedes the rules of total competition.

Prosperity and Innovation

Political stability and economic reforms are crucial for obtaining the benefits of international marketing. The field gives hope to countries that have been "in the dark" by offering better job prospects and improved skills. It augurs for more certainty in the future and enhances standards of living worldwide. International marketing might become the facilitator of a golden era in human history. Many products would not be economically viable without a global market. International marketing rewards excellence, accelerating innovation, and development. People have more opportunities to present their ideas and show their competitiveness to a wider audience. International marketing leverages the capabilities and resources that exist, lets us learn continuously and endows us with much more enthusiasm.

> "People also are changing their views of the international arena, particularly in a time when terrorism imposes daily reminders on us."

Culture

International marketing helps us to better understand our fellow human beings. Homogenization of cultures does not indicate that our aptitudes, likes, and behaviors would be the same. Rather, we would accept cultural differences and adapt them to our own culture, making us an amalgamation of different cultures. Global markets force companies and their employees to learn about other cultures and to develop relationships with "foreigners." This way, people get more exposure to various cultures, which leads to changes in the human character. International marketing enables individuals think thoughts that are wider ranging, developing many of us into a better person.

Fairness

Nations that trade are more interdependent. With merchandise promoted internationally, people can now easily make price comparisons, reducing selective exploitation due to knowledge monopolies. Markets have a watchdog role to play to ensure that exploitation does not occur. There is a market conscience!

Such a conscience results from the greater understanding that consumers develop about the consequences of their buying decisions on others. The information boom makes it easier for markets to deliver on their supervisory role. Markets themselves are a form of democracy. Consumer support will reinforce societally desirable firm behavior and punish acts that are deemed socially unacceptable. In sum, there are many positive vistas about international marketing—most of them far reaching and crucial for the further development of society. Thankfully, executives realize that international marketing has little to do with the soliciting phone call that interrupts dinner, but rather see it as contributing to a better quality of life. Bravo!

But, of course, that is not all. There are also fears and challenges emanating from international marketing. We can do better. I will address these negatives later. Until then, please send me your perspectives on international marketing. You can help us all to learn more.

Business Not As Usual

International Marketers Need to Seek More Solid Footing

We have been reporting regularly on the results of our study, conducted with **American Marketing Association** sponsorship in 2008 and 2009, which examined long-term emerging trends in international business. In the study, we employed a Delphi approach, using three rounds of assessment, argument, and re-argument to create agreement or define areas of

---

With C. Skuba. Originally published in the *AMA Marketing Management*, Summer 2010. Used with permission of Michael R. Czinkota and the *AMA Marketing Management*.

dissent on issues among international marketing experts from Europe, Asia, Africa, and the Americas, who are active in business, policy, and research. What our experts anticipated begins to resonate as international marketers seek more solid footing in 2010.

A Look in the Mirror

In the face of increasing pressures from a wide variety of active stakeholders, corporations will need to undergo substantial internal and external evaluation of issues and approaches that had been taken for granted. Corporate structures, functional priorities, accounting systems, ethnocentric orientations, transparency, executive compensation, ethical conduct, and practices in corporate social responsibility and sustainability will all be subject to increased scrutiny and public pressure. What contributes to value and what is excessive—and therefore inappropriate?

The current backlash against high executive remuneration in the United States is symptomatic of what the Delphi panel expected. This backlash will continue. Executive compensation will again be judged in comparison with average pay levels, which may well lead to pay raises for those at middle and lower levels. At the same time, the higher education of future business leaders will introduce more dimensions of morality, ascetics and long-term orientation in their missions. With the crucial input from business schools, a new class of trained and dedicated managers needs to emerge who will become the standard bearers of better global business management practices.

Reducing costs and rooting out inefficient practices will be even more paramount for international marketers. Eliminating overhead and reducing distractions from noncore, internal business functions will occur. Marketers will seek to reduce overloaded rosters of marketing services agencies and eliminate or cut back on the redundancies in strategic planning and creative processes.

Responsibility Expectations

Consumers and governments will come to expect expanded practice of corporate social responsibility as *de rigueur*. Strong corporations will take a very proactive stance with their corporate social responsibility programs and standards of ethical conduct, in order to hold on to the goodwill that has been so laboriously built. As the case of Toyota has shown, such goodwill, created over decades, can deteriorate within months.

Annual corporate social responsibility reports, corporate citizenship reports, and sustainability reports are now common practices among most large global corporations, whereas they were rare a decade ago. While some smaller companies may not have fully accepted the necessity of this kind of reporting, the demands of stakeholders from around the globe will increasingly make corporate responsibility a common core international businesses strategy. Corporations will increasingly develop measurements for progress in areas covering environmental concerns, energy consumption, carbon emissions, water use, chemical residues, labor practices, responsible consumption, nutrition, and general health concerns.

Some companies will find global social concerns to be an opportunity for both responsibility and profit. There is a growing segment of international consumers who are willing to back up their moral and ecological convictions with a willingness to direct or even increase their expenditure patterns. Using a more strategic approach to social involvement, global marketers have recognized competitive advantage in products and programs that also benefit countries and communities. In the area of sustainability, some companies have seized upon these issues to develop core strategies for long-term growth. The crucial managerial contribution arises when various important social and business goals conflict. Making the right long-term decisions is where managers earn their money.

A New Impetus

Most experts agree that (business) trends are even more important to business strategy than they were only a few years ago. Keeping on top of global trends with a focus on long-term profitable growth will be vital to success. A look at the business plans of the top global marketers confirms the importance of emerging markets as drivers of significant growth. For example, population increase and urbanization in these markets are reshaping international marketing strategy. Coca-Cola, Danone, and Nestlé increasingly market nutrition rather than just food.

Keeping on top of global trends with a focus on long-term profitable growth will be vital to success.

The Delphi panelists expect a greater emphasis on the markets provided by "second-tier cities," which are large cities not yet in the political or economic spotlight—particularly in Russia, China, and India.

Smaller firms can also benefit from the globalization of markets by seeking opportunity in niche markets, especially those neglected or abandoned by the large players. As large corporations seek economies of scale, smaller players may discover important customer needs that have been left underserved and valuable brands that may have been jettisoned by the giants. Of course, smaller players will need to seek efficiencies through strategic alliances and other joint efforts to compete globally. They will also be heavily dependent on industry and government efforts to establish open markets and global standards.

Nations, countries, regions and cities will also pursue niche strategies as they will further specialize in the development of industry clusters. Firms will open subsidiaries, research and development centers and representative offices in order to take advantage of the proximity to competitors, suppliers, customers and research providers. Governments will seek advantage through clusters and place greater emphasis on the special educational needs of the workforce in those industrial clusters.

With most dynamic growth coming from emerging markets, the more developed economies seem destined for slower growth patterns. Inevitably, those who do not participate in economic expansion will become frustrated and seek relief through government remedies. Government has again become and will remain an important factor in international marketing. The dangers of an insular focus lurk. Changing times will require strong leadership from the public sector and corporations to avoid the easy, but wrong, answer of protectionism.

Encourage Sharing of
Local Practices

If Only Global Firms Knew What They Know
About Local Marketing

A global firm wants to develop local loyalty programs. It might happen that some of its own country's organizations already have well-established programs in place. Yet country A's staff is unaware that a loyalty program already has been built in country B, so they're not asking. The country B subsidiary doesn't know that country A is in need of help, so they're not telling. Often, country marketing managers may accumulate impressive

With M. Schrader. Originally published in the *AMA Marketing Management*, December 13, 2010. Used with permission of Michael R. Czinkota and the *AMA Marketing Management*.

knowledge, but the firm does not. Synergies from internationalization fail to materialize.

Global firms often don't know what they know. They miss out on the essence of internationalism: developing and using information on a global basis. Knowledge is only accidentally shared throughout the firm.

Today, many small and medium-sized firms service multiple markets abroad. For them, marketing knowledge that is locked up in a single country is a waste of resources and a limitation on competitiveness.

Cultural differences between countries may influence the way local best-marketing practices are being developed and shared. For example, countries with a high degree of uncertainty avoidance may tend to adopt new marketing ideas later (e.g., use of social media). Also, the enthusiasm in sharing marketing knowledge itself may be affected by cultural predispositions. Research indicates that the dissemination and cross-fertilization of (marketing) knowledge is more intense in collectivist societies (e.g., China and Indonesia) than in individualistic countries (e.g., the United States and United Kingdom).

But the issues that unite us are much more frequent than those that separate us. Interaction between corporate units will provide the opportunity for progress. A global firm will inevitably face conditions where some countries are more advanced than others. But thinking about gradual convergence encourages the sharing of valuable insights internally across the globe.

If marketing decisions are taken at headquarters and country organizations are mainly executing instructions, the creation of unique marketing knowledge is less likely. In decentralized and highly differentiated firms, country organizations have a high degree of autonomy. Here, the accumulation of information that is worthwhile to share is much more likely. Of course, trade-offs need to be made in the context of overall corporate and environmental constraints. For example, a pharmaceutical firm that considers the guarding of trade secrets and tight enforcement of uniformity as crucial to its competitive advantage is much less likely to encourage the individualization of programs.

To succeed in sharing marketing knowledge, global firms need to maintain an understanding and inventory of what's going on in country and regional operations. Global headquarters often lack such insight. They have an understanding of how the country is performing based on the yardsticks of general measures, but they don't know the details of the subsidiaries' marketing successes (or failures).

To collect and spread marketing knowledge, firms require dedicated individuals who continuously collect information from local operations and serve as knowledge hubs. It should not be the job for everyone.

The marketing knowledge champions should be individuals with significant experience and a broad network within the firm. Ideally, they worked in different countries before taking on their role. There is no need to have all the champions centrally located—as long as the knowledge is centrally acceptable.

Developing best-practice knowledge in marketing is not a question of market size or degree of market industrialization. The knowledge champions must identify countries with marketing best practices. There is no need to always look to the "big fishes" (i.e., organizations in large and established countries, such as the United States or Germany). Smaller countries and emerging markets are able to develop innovative marketing solutions as well. The Czech subsidiary of a global cell phone provider developed new solutions retaining existing customers. Often, it is primarily the creativity and sense of entrepreneurship of the local marketing staff rather than sheer numbers that turn a country into an internal marketing leader.

New ways of communication and interaction facilitate local marketing knowledge sharing. It is also useful to encourage the interaction between individuals from different environments. For example, there is no harm in encouraging staff to visit their counterparts abroad when on an international vacation.

Firms need a culture in which asking for foreign advice, as well as supporting others, is perceived as beneficial.

Once local marketing best practices are identified, knowledge sharing can be achieved one to one or through workshops, Web exchange or university courses specifically designed for disseminating marketing knowledge.

There is also the opportunity to use case study competitions, which elucidate a marketing approach used to overcome a tricky situation. The information bank created by such information can be crucial for subsequent analysis and teaching.

The digitization of information and possibilities of electronic communication facilitates global knowledge sharing. Data and information are available better and faster across the globe than ever before, and can provide for international cross-fertilization. To avoid complexity and information overload, it is important to offer easy-to-use search terms, simple delete functions and meaningful keywords.

A fundamental prerequisite to achieving local marketing knowledge sharing is persuading the marketing staff of the benefits of doing so. Firms need a culture in which asking for foreign advice, as well as supporting others, is perceived as beneficial. Country organizations may have different maturity levels. While beginner countries receive a "first aid kit" and reduce their risk of failure, advanced countries can position themselves within the firm as front-runners yet also be poised to learn from their colleagues. For example, consumer goods firms in advanced nations can still learn from some of the approaches used successfully in "bottom-of-the-pyramid" nations.

It helps to encourage conversation between marketers—both domestic and international. A narrow focus may lead to insufficient information or scarce opportunities. Once there is an exposure to things international, the interest may grow rapidly.

Good marketing usually means that specific marketing knowledge is developed locally. Best local practices are required knowledge for a multinational firm. To make this knowledge transparent and accessible for colleagues in other countries is indispensable. Unlock this knowledge. Start with assigning global knowledge champions and identifying local marketing best practices. And then spread the word.

Medical Tourism is a Gift to U.S. Health Care

Consumers and providers of medical services in the U.S. often search for opportunities to cut costs. Increasingly, it is possible to find low-priced care alternatives abroad. In the heated debate about health-care changes, a key aspect is, of course, the expense of providing such care. The emergence and efficiency of medical tourism may well help bridge the chasm between costs and revenues, and between desire and ability.

Already today, prospective patients are traveling in ever-increasing numbers to such exotic destinations as Brazil and Thailand in search

Originally published in *The Providence Journal*, December 25, 2009. Used with permission of Michael R. Czinkota and *The Providence Journal*.

of high-quality care at a fraction of the cost. Sarah Murray reports in *The Financial Times* that the medical-tourism industry has grown by about 14 percent from 2007 to 2009, and is predicted to expand at 35 percent annually by 2010. By 2012, it is predicted to serve more than 1.6 million international patients.

The rationale behind the industry's development is straightforward customer's search for convenience. If comfort and coziness can also become part of the outcome, the much the better. Now, however, there are additional new key players in the U.S. government and the health-care industry, who may reconsider their previous lack of support for medical tourism.

A medical procedure at an Indian or Chinese hospital can cost 70 percent less than what a patient would pay in the West. For patients from countries with public health-care systems, such as Canada and Britain, medical travel is already often motivated by the desire to reduce or avoid current delays and waiting periods leading up to their procedures.

The growth in medical tourism is a boon for health-care providers in the developing world. For example, reports Murray, in India the sector is projected to expand by 30 percent annually from 2009 to 2015, which may make it worth $4.4 billion. Increasingly, internationally accredited medical centers are emerging in countries such as the Philippines and Mexico, eager to accommodate the ever-growing stream of Western patients. Governments in the developing world are beginning to invest in support infrastructure to promote their health-care services internationally. As their industry's medical skills increase, their comparative advantage will attract more customers from abroad.

For those concerned about quality, the increased flow of international students to learning centers of global excellence may ease some of these worries. Also, the existence of international accreditation standards can increase the confidence and comfort that institutions and patients can have in institutions abroad. Furthermore, as time passes there will increasingly be a track record that can be checked and compared. In addition, there may well be better legal protection of patients and providers abroad.

Medical tourism also gives rise to new industry growth. New companies are formed that assist patients with scheduling their procedures overseas. They help clients with planning their trips and offer in-country support, such as airport transfers, after-care arrangements, hospital liaisons and dispute mediation. Most of these companies started out catering to individual clients. However, they are now expanding to offer their services to meet businesses demand. With the rising costs of providing employee health care, more corporations are searching for alternatives to home-country care, and insurance may become more willing to cover procedures conducted abroad. While the health-care-plan alternatives are debated, its cost continues to soar. More coverage and coverage of more patients definitely will mean higher cost, if other dimensions are not changed. In addition, the demand for elective procedures such as cosmetic and dental surgery continues to rise. In light of all these financial pressures, international trade in medical tourism may well offer the tipping point, which allows acceptance of more coverage while restraining costs.

The Two Faces of International Marketing

Effective Marketing and Ethical Practices
Must Exist Together

We both are dyed-in-the-wool international marketers.

Our last column explained our fervent belief in the contributions of international marketing to a better quality of life. Yet there are also fears and challenges emanating from the field and its activities. International

---

With C. Skuba. Originally published in the *AMA Marketing Management*, Winter 2011. Used with permission of Michael R. Czinkota and the *AMA Marketing Management*.

marketing brings both good and bad to the global marketplace, and has come to embody the notion of contradiction to modern thinkers, just like the Roman god Janus who had two faces. Exploitation of factory workers by global apparel brands exemplifies the negative consequences of globalization, but that is really more of an operations and management issue (except for the risk and impact of negative publicity on the brand). With the recent dramatic expansion of international marketing to new audiences in the developing world, there are serious social impacts that need consideration. Here are our thoughts on those, calibrated by input from global executives.

Encounter of the Unexpected

Janus was not only a god of contradiction but a god whose countenance the Romans put on doors and gates as a symbol of transition. There are many who, in times of transition, have come new to market, and even new to marketing. New dimensions have made life more complex, both for marketers and those who are being marketed to. For example, some slogans offered routinely to markets with a public experienced with marketing, such as "you may have won a new car," may be interpreted quite differently by newcomers. Their high expectations may lead to disappointments and even hostility. Because marketers are the initiators of new practices, it is their responsibility to avoid causing harm.

Distorting Aspirations

As economic growth in emerging markets allows millions of people to enter the middle class, it brings great new opportunities for them to improve the quality of their lives. It also exposes them to the challenge of rising aspirations with limited income. New international consumers must learn how to manage their aspirations as they experience emotional marketing appeals for products and services that might not be considered practical or "good for them."

In a chapter titled "Ethical Lapses of Marketers" in Jagdish Sheth and Rajendra Sisodia's book, *Does Marketing Need Reform: Fresh Perspectives on the Future* (M.E. Sharpe, 2006), my good friend Philip Kotler posed two dimensions of "the marketing dilemma" for all marketing: (1) What if the customer wants something that is not good for him or her? (2) What if the product or service, while good for the customer, is not good for society or other groups?

How consumers, marketers and societies manage that dilemma in international markets will need to be resolved on a country-by-country basis.

Coping with Culture

All too often, cultures are insufficiently studied or wrongly interpreted. It might seem that responsiveness to cultural differences should be second nature to marketers and therefore virtually reflexive. However, cultural differences continue to challenge marketers and can negatively affect the marketplace. Many times, disregarding local idiosyncrasies is like the introduction of a destructive virus on a culture.

Though there is frequent talk about how we understand each other so much better than in the past, the reality looks different. The actual overlap between societies is typically very miniscule. There may be a number of Chinese industry leaders who have been to the United States and have developed a clear understanding of America and Americans, but they represent a very small fraction of the Chinese populace. The average Chinese may knowledgably understand as much about Columbus, Ohio, as the average Buckeye State resident knows about Tianjin. The consequence of that limitation is a danger of misunderstandings and susceptibility to hostility.

Winner Takes All

One key Western marketing dimension is the glory of victory in competition. Such an adherence to victory often means that there is no mercy for the vanquished. Not everywhere are such approaches supported, desired or accepted. Often, the goal becomes for the victor to mend fences, reinvigorate a feeling of togetherness and provide a cause for standing together. In many societies it is expected that one does not take advantage of what could be done, but rather consensually do what ought to be done.

Such context makes it far less acceptable to practice what we have called "vampire marketing," where the airline or hotel extracts blood-sucking prices for additional services or products from its captive audience after the major purchase decision has been made. Perhaps Western marketers can learn valuable lessons from this context and consequently make themselves more valuable to their customers.

> "As international marketers voraciously pursue opportunity, they will also encounter fierce local competition and instant copying of good ideas."

Who Is on the Pedestal?

Particularly in the United States, we think of the individual as the key component of society. But such a perspective is not uniformly taken around the world. For example, in socialist or tribal societies it is typically the group that receives preference over the individual. Society can also be seen as the key shaper of the individual. Or perhaps the family is accorded top billing. In such cases, just imagine how different emphases in making financial decisions can be re-interpreted in various settings. What may be corruption and bribery to some may turn out to be filial devotion to others. With the strict administration of the U.S. Foreign Corrupt Practices Act and the new, more stringent U.K. anti-bribery law about to take effect, there may be harsh consequences to businesses and individuals who are not attentive to the laws governing that contradiction.

It's Not Personal

Distance makes the heart grow fonder. But in international marketing, distance can also mean abdication of responsibility. Marketers sometimes clearly demonstrate their desire not to know. As developing nations develop greater expectations of corporate social responsibility and create new legal requirements, irresponsible marketers may encounter a less tolerant face in host countries. Though the chairman of the multinational corporation may feel removed from local issues, be assured that the locals take all of the firm's actions very personally.

Whose Idea Is It anyway?

As international marketers voraciously pursue opportunity, they will also encounter fierce local competition and instant copying of good ideas. Intellectual property rights violations are rampant in many parts of the developing world. These not only harm the international marketer but also the consumers who purchase defective products. Think of the consumer who needs treatment for a critical illness and receives a fake drug.

We can use Janus as a god of contradictions and transitions, but we cannot turn to him for guidance in morality, ethics or even law. International marketers will confront dilemmas and challenges. How well they pursue the conjunction of highly effective marketing and ethical practices will inevitably be reflected in the loyalty of customers and the judgment of host governments.

Scenarios Key to Strategic Plans of International Marketing Managers

As the reliability and value of pinpoint forecasts in a changing world become doubtful, scenario construction, which considers various alternative futures, has become an effective tool for international marketing managers to use in strategic planning.

Originally published in the *Marketing News*, May 30, 1980. Used with permission of Michael R. Czinkota and the *Marketing News*.

Forecasting changes in the environment, recognizing their importance, and adapting to them creatively have always been the daily bread of marketing professionals.

But since today's changes occur more frequently, more rapidly—and are more severe in their impact, the past seems to have lost much of its value as a predictor of the future. Who really knows how many more Irans there will be in the years to come?

What is considered stable today may not only be altered in the future, but may be completely overturned. Governments freeze assets. Sales volumes in certain countries drop to zero in a matter of weeks. The sentiments of whole populations, consistent over decades, reverse completely within months. All of these changes highlight the complexities which international marketing managers face today.

Since these developments point toward increased international hazards, one simple-minded alternative for risk-averting managers is the termination of *all* international activities.

HOWEVER, BUSINESSES will not achieve long-run success by engaging only in (close to) risk-free actions. Besides, various other factors make the survival of international business highly probable.

International markets continue to be very profitable, as a quick look at the *Fortune* 500 shows. Overseas markets help cushion the slack in domestic sales resulting from recessionary or adverse market conditions and are often crucial to corporate solvency, a fact to which Ford Motor Co. can attest.

U.S. companies also gain valuable foreign experience from international markets, which helps them compete more successfully with foreign firms operating in the U.S. domestic market.

Finally, international activities are necessary to compensate for foreign commodity inflows into the U.S. economy and to at least contribute to a favorable balance of trade. Therefore, an inherent economic motivation exists for international trade. This will hopefully result in government support, although such support may manifest itself only in the reduction of obstacles of international trade.

Despite these motivations, international activities cannot be initiated on the spur of the moment. As with any major company activity, internationalism warrants long-range planning, careful preparation, and gradual development.

RATHER THAN viewing international activities only as a part of the operational area (a pitfall to which many firms succumb), marketing management must take a strategic view of the future of its international expansion.

This strategy, as mentioned earlier, can use scenario construction as a guiding force. In the development of a general scenario framework, three main macroparameters seem to exist.

The future world will continue to consist of developed countries (DCs) and lesser developed countries (LDCs). Some theoreticians argue that the gap among these two groups will diminish, while others hold that the gap will widen. Both arguments, however, lead to the conclusion that the gap will endure.

We also will witness growing nationalism manifesting itself in various ways, such as efforts to become technologically autonomous, refusal to communicate in heretofore "acceptable" international languages, etc.

There will also be increasing pressure by the LDCs on the DCs to help improve the fortunes of the LDCs, as the North-South dialogue amply demonstrates.

Although these three parameters are by no means exhaustive in describing world needs, they help define the boundaries of the future. They are of sufficient impact to warrant the design of four alternative scenarios with highly relevant implications for international marketing managers.

1. COOPERATION: The LDCs and DCs will work together. DCs will relinquish part of their economic power to LDCs, thus contributing activity to their progress through a sharing of resources and technology. These subsidies will aid the LDCs, but will result in a general flattening of the standard of living in the more affluent DCs.

2. CONFRONTATION: Due to an unwillingness to sufficiently share resources and technology (or excessively, depending on this point of view), LDCs and DCs will be pitted against each other. Frequent hostilities will result in high expenditures in the defense sector and bring about severe restrictions and inhibitions to international trade.

3. ISOLATION: Increased cooperation within the LDCs and DCs takes place, while both groups form blocs which remain basically isolated from each other. Each group is faced with different problems, to which group-unique solutions are sought and found.

4. DISPERSION: While some nations remain with the LDC/DC framework, others find new values on which to orient themselves. Such orientation may focus on religion, quality of life, and so forth, and will result in a diminishing or abolition of currently held business values. The recent changes in Iran may be an exemplification of the beginning of such a development.

Although the framework and the scenarios considered are quite general, important marketing implications can be drawn. But due to the generality, the implications are strategic rather than tactical.

Regardless of whether international exchange continues freely, all scenarios result in a reduction of resource availability, due to unilateral resource shifts, cutoffs from some markets, or increased defense expenditures.

Domestically and internationally, the direction of product demand will be less luxury and more necessity oriented. The meaning of frugality will blossom to currently unknown dimensions in the future.

General product development will need to be carried out on two different levels. There will need to be products for DCs and products for LDCs. Needs and wants will differ too greatly to allow current product adjustment or adaptation policies to be sufficient.

LESS DIRECT foreign investment will occur in order for the asset exposure of firms to be reduced. If undertaken, such investments will accumulate within the country blocs.

The investments will also be concentrated in labor-intensive rather than capital-intensive industries and will be mainly service-oriented, thus not only using the comparative advantage of LDCs but also reducing risk and loss from sudden change.

More foreign investment will be through joint ventures, with firms from DCs contributing the expertise in a step-wise fashion and firms from LDCs supplying the venture capital.

These developments will require new management styles aimed at reducing and resolving completely new intraorganizational goal conflicts.

In line with risk reduction, the future will have more firms concentrating on exporting as their main (and only) international activity since it represents less risk of total asset loss while having the capability of responding rapidly to change.

SINCE SUCH export activities will result in less capital tie-ups within firms, greater quantities can be exported to more countries, making firms less vulnerable to sudden local disruptions.

However, because of the strict exporting focus the profitability of international activities will decline. Thus, the importance of designing cost-effective international logistics and export support systems will increase.

These directional shifts represent only a few of the major changes which will have to be monitored as part of international strategy development. As tomorrow draws nearer, more information will enable management to focus on tactical decisions.

New Opportunity Dawns in the Japanese Market

The Japanese market holds much promise for U.S. firms as new forms of doing business evolve. Mail-order and non-store retailing are becoming part of the daily consumer landscape.

Likely to be even more prominent are the capabilities to conduct business in "market space" rather than the traditional marketplace. The global emergence of electronic commerce offers alternatives that bypass many traditional entry barriers into Japan.

According to our international study of Japanese distribution strategy, which was published by the American Marketing Association in the

With M. Kotabe. Originally published in the *Journal of Commerce*, March 1, 2000. Used with permission of Michael R. Czinkota and the *Journal of Commerce*.

winter issue of *Marketing Management*, U.S. firms are better positioned to take advantage of electronic commerce opportunities than are Japanese members of the distribution system. This is because Japanese industry lags in its implementation of information technology.

Why aren't more U.S. firms in the Japanese market? The answer lies in the numerous Japanese market barriers, key of which are the keiretsu, a term that describes the set of intimate relationships among Japanese suppliers and manufacturers that lock up the Japanese distribution system.

These practices, however, are beginning to change. This is primarily because of Japan's decade-long battle with its worst postwar recession. Many keiretsu companies have experienced severe asset deflation and lost control of member companies' shares. Many traditional barriers to entry into Japan's distribution sector persist. Relative to other markets, real-estate prices, labor costs and freight charges remain high. The need also remains to offer high levels of service, substantial financing and frequent rebates.

Other entry difficulties stem from Japanese consumers' high-quality expectations, an increase in bureaucratic red tape as a result of under-staffed Japanese government offices, the country's inadequate import infrastructure, and delays in processing patent, trademark and other intellectual property rights. How, then, should U.S. and other foreign firms cope with Japan's market barriers and improve their ability to penetrate the Japanese market? The key: better business strategy.

Trade negotiations with the Japanese government may help some-what, but the use of seasoned business practices is the foremost means to achieving market penetration.

Such practices consist of thorough market research, product adaptation to local expectations, emphasis on service orientation, collaborative ventures, a long-term orientation and an alert responsiveness to changes in the market. Also important is the development of an Export Complaint Management (ECM) system that shows customers how to complain, where to complain, to whom to complain and encourages them to complain. An ECM system captures complaints and uses them to progressively improve products and processes—an approach crucial to success in Japan.

U.S. firms will improve their foothold in the Japanese market mainly through direct investment, rather than exports. Lack of such investment may serve as a self-fulfilling prophecy for a lack of success. If being there sends the signals of reliability, long-term outlook, and corporate commitment of foreign firms, then an export-only strategy may be seen as communicating the obverse.

Traditional trade negotiations are losing their relevance when they concentrate on bureaucratic impediments directly controlled by the government. They focus mainly on issues that are of only marginal importance to overall business success in Japan.

A new focus is required on business models beyond trade, such as foreign direct investment, licensing and franchising, as well as the protection of intellectual property rights. These options require foreign firms to become more Japanese in orientation and location, enabling them to compete the Japanese way. Conversely, change will not become entrenched in Japan until the country adopts more American practices. Some of these include increased consumer optimism and spending and less obsession with low-interest personal savings.

The emergence of a nimble Japanese venture capital market would also have dramatically positive effects. Mutual adjustment that makes us more alike will benefit both the United States and Japan.

Washington Needs a Marketing Approach to Trade

The emerging trade policy of the Clinton administration emphasizes market access and increases in foreign imports. Particularly in U.S.–Japanese trade relations, preliminary discussions have focused on managed trade, self-imposed quotas and government-mandated trade-imbalance adjustments.

Yet, the facts show that such approaches are inappropriate. They would distort market forces and send the wrong signals to both producers and customers, mark the abandonment of multiculturalism, create the danger of a backlash in which other countries implement similar approaches, and still not increase U.S. jobs and economic activity measurably.

Originally published in *The Asian Wall Street Journal*, June 28, 1993. Used with permission of Michael R. Czinkota and *The Asian Wall Street Journal*.

Instead of wasting governmental effort and funds on such an approach, United States needs to become marketing-oriented in its trade policy by understanding foreign demand and helping U.S. industry excel in satisfying such demand.

The Wood Example

U.S. trade negotiations with Japan in the wood-products industry and subsequent results provide an excellent example. The U.S. General Accounting Office reports that for more than a decade the U.S. has been negotiating with the Japanese government so that more U.S. solid wood products can enter the Japanese market, particularly in the construction field. High-level meetings, ongoing negotiations, government financial support and industry demonstration products were to achieve that goal.

After all these efforts, much has been accomplished. Japanese building codes—which, due to fire-code provisions had prohibited construction of multistory wooden buildings—were changed. Product certification was made less costly and less complicated. Certification authority, previously the exclusive purview of the Ministry of Construction, was delegated to foreign testing organizations such as the American Plywood Association in the United States. Japan's tariffs were lowered for processed solid wood products—for softwood plywood to 10% from 16%, for glue-laminated beams to 4% from 15%. To top it all off, the Foreign Agricultural Service spent close to $18 million to promote U.S. wood-product sales to Japan.

Why U.S. Companies Lag

With all these successes in hand, one would expect U.S. leadership in the market for solid wood products in Japan, together with rapid employment growth back home. Instead, the market leadership belongs to the Canadians, and the job increases in the United States have been marginal.

There are several reasons for this situation. First, Canadian firms were much quicker than U.S. companies to take advantage of the changes. Canadian firms obtained certification faster, and were more aggressive in their marketing. They understand the different specifications and grades of wood products in Japan, they pay attention to product quality and appearance, and demonstrate more commitment to market and after-sales service requirements such as the development of manuals in Japanese.

By contrast, U.S. firms tend to provide their information in English, tend to be less reliable as long-range suppliers, show little interest in after-sales service and don't meet Japanese quality and appearance standards.

Of even greater importance is the U.S. disregard of the Japanese market. American companies try to sell what they produce to the Japanese, rather than producing what the Japanese want to buy. The largest portion of Japan's market for solid wood products is in post-and-beam construction, not in timber frames. Only 7% of new wooden homes are built by using U.S.–type two-by-four products. Most other wooden housing construction uses four-by-four posts and boards for framing and is based on a three-by-six-foot module that fits the standard-sized tatami mats that cover the floors. In other words, U.S. companies have focused all of their energies on increasing their penetration of the smallest part of the market, and have done so with only limited success.

Third, those U.S. firms that do attempt to adjust their products to Japanese market requirements encounter major problems in financing the new equipment and longer export payment terms. They also run into human-resource problems when trying to meet Japanese quality standards or searching for international business expertise.

Policy Keys

What needs to be done differently? As Washington becomes more involved in trade, it should do so in a market-oriented way. The key drivers for U.S. trade policy need to be:

- A focus on market opportunities that make a difference; go for the big ones.
- Identification of the needs and desires of foreign customers; marketing something they want is much easier than trying to sell what we have.
- Industry commitment to government market-opening approaches; firms make the sales, not governments.
- A link between trade policy and domestic assistance to firms planning to go abroad; entry potential abroad is useless unless U.S. firms are given the capability to take advantage of it—be it through information, production refinements or financing.

Washington needs to explicitly recognize that the times are over when the United States opened foreign markets simply for the well being of the world. Though it might be a delightful side effect to also see other nations' trade increase after the United States has broken down trade barriers, the key focus rests on American jobs. Second, the United States needs to understand that public funds are scarce, as is its capacity to negotiate and its capability to achieve negotiation success. Washington therefore can no longer afford to invest funds and government attention (and generate friction) solely to right wrongs or for the sake of fairness. Rather, funds should only be expended if the market is large enough to warrant attention and government actions are fully supported and followed up by industry.

American trade policy needs to be focused on those issues that make a meaningful difference in terms of jobs and economic activity. After all, that is what funds government operations, provides taxes, reduces adjustment expenditures and pays for health care.

U.S. and Japan Must Find a New Common Ground

With the Clinton-Hosokawa trade summit having ended on a discordant note, followed by threats of trade sanctions, Washington's annual bashing of the Japanese seems to have started on cue. But this time differs from the last 10 bashings. Now it's not just Congress but also a determined administration that has taken the lead, declaring that a decade of dillydallying is enough. Yes, we need new actions, but not the ones taken now—they are just plain bad policy.

Originally published in *The Asian Wall Street Journal*, February 28, 1994. Used with permission of Michael R. Czinkota and *The Asian Wall Street Journal*.

Pushing Japan hard on changes makes sense. To do so now, by demanding quantitative goals and expecting immediate results, doesn't. Prime Minister Morihiro Hosokawa has introduced major change in Japan, which will strengthen the market orientation of the Japanese economy and U.S.–Japanese relations. By asking him in the middle of crucial domestic battles to make U.S. trade his only focus, the administration is aiding his opposition. By doing the asking in a highly public forum with a U.S. position of immovable toughness, the administration neglects the cultural importance of saving face and unnecessarily raises public expectations. It is the demagoguery of trade hawks raising and then shattering high expectations that results in growing disappointment and resentment.

Three more facets make the current approach malodorous. First, demanding that the Japanese government ensure more private purchases from the United States requires government planning and control of the economy—an approach proven unsuccessful with the demise of the centrally planned Soviet Union. Second, punitive tariffs betray producers and consumers in the United States through reduced choices and increased prices. Finally, demanding bilateral results and taking unilateral action slights the very General Agreement on Tariffs and Trade that negotiators from around the world just spent seven years reviving.

A New Foundation

Yet, after more than a decade of limited progress, of mutual bickering and increasing political heat, the basic premise of changing the footing of U.S.–Japanese trade relations is sound. Japan and the United States have lost much of their former commonality of purpose. The dramatic changes sweeping through Eastern Europe and the Soviet Union have vanquished a major threat that previously tied the two countries closely together. Now that Japan and the United States aren't seeing red anymore, both are trying to decide how much or whether they still need each other. Close-up inspection without a mutual bond can be detrimental; it discovers the warts and the flab without the soothing effect of the relationship. It is important that Japan and the United States again find a common purpose that will build and develop their relationship on a more elevated plane. The former Soviet empire can still be the catalyst that moves them in that direction.

By working together, the United States and Japan can set the stage for a new integration of the world economy. In both countries, enough is known about competition, about collaboration, about market opportunities and market adjustments, to make a direct contribution to Eastern integration and help overcome ingrained systemic differences.

Take one area where such collaboration could start—the field of logistics and distribution. Both the United States and Japan excel here. The total cost of distribution in both countries is running close to 11% of GNP. By 1995, experts predict, 40% of shipments in U.S. companies will be under a just-in-time, quick-response regime.

In contrast, distribution costs in Eastern Europe and Russia are well above 30% of GNP. Governments are battling poor supply lines, nonexistent distribution and service centers, limited rolling stock and insufficient transportation systems. Producers know nothing about benchmarking, inventory carrying cost, store assortment efficiencies, and replenishment techniques. Only poorly understood are the need for information development and exchange systems, for integrated distributor–supplier alliances and for efficient communication systems such as electronic data interchange.

Benefits Outweigh Concerns

Imagine the difference collaboration between the United States and Japan could make in taking on this problem area. Imagine the effects in terms of market growth and welfare gains. Compare these benefits to the problem areas forcing the two countries apart. Washington and Tokyo cannot afford to sacrifice the gains of collaboration on the altar of narrow trade concerns.

The United States and Japan have the opportunity to exercise leadership with a long-term perspective. Both countries have a new commonality of interest in the need to bring the formerly centrally-planned economies into the fold of market forces, making them safe for national security and attractive for economic security. Both countries, have much to offer to this process: knowledge, technology, information, capital, enthusiasm and markets. Both also have a lot at stake: they need a world safe from nuclear banditry; they need new markets that are growing; they need a unifying goal that encourages collaboration; they need a rousing battle cry in favor of competition. The United States and Japan aren't just interdependent on each other, but also the world. They need to see trade conflicts in perspective and recognize their relative importance given other burning issues. Their interests haven't grown apart, they are converging. The two sides just need a higher plateau to see more of the horizon.

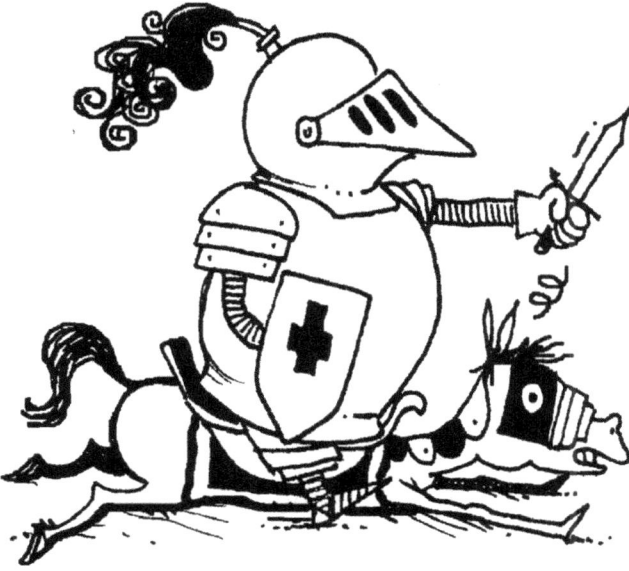

On Transitions

Middle East Instability: Thoughts for Managers

How does the newly visible instability in the Middle East affect international managers and their firms? What strategic adjustments are needed for managers to cope with possibly hostile business environments abroad?

Business is more interconnected today than ever before. Specifically, global commerce today relies on layers of suppliers, distributors, and customers, located all around the world. Such extensive networks increase firms' exposure to events that occur at distant locations. Even

---

With G. Knight. Originally published in *The Korea Times*, February 7, 2011. Used with permission of Michael R. Czinkota and *The Korea Times*.

firms that rely little on international business may depend on the receipt of imported goods. We have asked several hundred international corporations and their managers about their responses to crises. What international businesses repercussions do we need to watch out for?

Managers respond not necessarily to reality, but to widespread perceptions of reality. In times of conflict, the "winner" may well be the side that most effectively communicates their victory.

If all anticipate major uncertainty, then times will be uncertain. If threats to personal fortunes are expected, then capital flight will take place. And therein turns the wheel of fortune—if enough believe in a condition, it may well become reality.

Though authoritarian regimes may have been able to minimize local terrorism, new instability may lead to ungoverned spaces. Civil unrest is a fertile breeding ground for the emergence of violence and terrorism. Thus, the instability we are witnessing overseas may give rise to "exogenous shocks" that threaten global supply chains, distribution channels, and other infrastructure that firms need to conduct their international operations.

Managers will adjust their planning activities—higher risks will be assumed not just in the disrupted locality, but globally. Lenders and insurance companies will expect higher premiums. The return-on-investment expectations for new investments will rise. As a result, global investment plans may be significantly delayed or even terminated.

Crises will disrupt local conditions and lead to unemployment. There may not be enough bread, and insufficient delivery of alimentation, leading to hungry masses. For the multinational firm it means there will be disruptions of global supply chains and distribution networks.

Crises typically also lead to a depression of buyer psychology and reduced consumption. Local markets may shrink, (just imagine possible effects on the Suez Canal, which handles 8 percent of global sea trade and over 2 million barrels of oil daily), and supplies of international markets will be reduced.

Accessing markets will be more difficult and less efficient. There is likely to be more security scrutiny, and increased exposure to perils when delivering goods to crisis zones. The safety cost of such deliveries may increase logistics expenses by up to 15 percent.

Firms will encounter rising transaction costs. Managers will need to find new suppliers, whose products will cost more. New shipping routes will be more expensive. Routine processes lose their routine since new participants in a new setting are inexperienced and prone to mistakes. Coordinating costs between suppliers and distributors are likely to surge.

Larger inventories will have to be held, particularly by companies with just-in-time systems, in order to assure flexibility and production continuity. These inventories will cost more money, with increases of 10 percent or more.

All of these changes add up. Smaller firms may withdraw from markets to avoid intolerable risk levels. For the U.S., the aim to double exports by 2014 will be in jeopardy. Rising costs of energy, food and commodities will affect inflation and levels of economic balance.

Consider today's U.S. current account, which measures all the inflows and outflows of the economy. Almost 25 percent of U.S. imports consist of oil. Even if one can stabilize import quantity, a higher price per barrel will further increase this burden.

Today, firms need a big-picture perspective, and choose between short-term gains and long-term success. Managers need to explore opportunities for collaboration, using a planning umbrella that considers customers, suppliers, and suppliers' suppliers.

In the wake of major shifts, firms need to become part of the solution. Businesses need to move away from focusing only on self-serving or localized concerns and ensure the survival of the organization by examining its long-term future fit within the societies where it operates.

Terrorism Preparedness: We Can Pay Now or Pay Later

International terrorists attack businesses far more than any other target, and when they strike, they aim to disrupt the flow of supply and demand and to destroy our way of life.

A survey of 642 global firms found that terrorism is the third most important concern to management, after energy prices and exchange-rate volatility. The companies surveyed reportedly spent on average about $147,000 on terrorism preparedness and hired about five new employees to deal with the issue. Yet many other corporations do not believe

---

Originally published in *The Japan Times*, November 28, 2005. Used with permission of Michael R. Czinkota and *The Japan Times*.

their shareholders would reward these investments, and therefore remain unprepared for the impact of terrorism.

With today's global competition, firms no longer have the luxury of just aiming for "survival" in the face of an emergency or a terror attack. Firms must offer continuity to their suppliers, their clients and their employees in order to inspire confidence in the relationship. Flexibility allows firms to recover more quickly in the aftermath of terrorism's direct and indirect consequences.

Preparedness is of key importance to any firm. For example, after hurricane Katrina, many displaced students and faculty members from New Orleans found continuity in Georgetown University classrooms immediately because contingency plans had been made. Even relatively small and local events can cause major dislocations. Suppliers can go out of business or have their facilities burn to the ground. Employees may be struck by illness or a labor dispute may halt shipments.

To safeguard the investment of shareholders and assure the viability of their firm, managers must prepare contingency plans that respond to system shocks. We have developed a model of corporate readiness for international terrorism that links people, activities and society, and identifies opportunities for improvement. We propose a model of the different levels of corporate readiness for international terrorism by linking the relationship among conditions, activities and people, and identifying the leverage points to initiate improvement and change. It also helps to evaluate policy approaches to emergency preparedness in general.

We start with a terrorist threat or incident that causes both direct and indirect effects. They trigger the actions of responders, who can be either internal or external to the firm. These responders and the media shape the information, experience and perception of society and the firm. One consequence is the creation of friction that slows down international business transactions.

The availability of resources and the firm's willingness to employ them affects the level of preparation. Managers typically are totally unprepared for the effects of terrorism on their firms, and are not willing to undertake any kind of investment. With sufficient input, managers change their attitude but are still not ready for any action. As concern grows, management searches for input such as checklists or audits. Eventually managers plan at a tactical and strategic level, and integrate stakeholders such as employees, suppliers, banks and legislators. Finally, management actually prepares the firm for terrorism by, for example, making provisions for emergency relocation of employees and ensure that they have employment, and that they get paid when the ATMs are down.

From a public-policy perspective we know that legislative preparation will be more advantageous than an overly rapid but unexamined response to a current emergency. Our model indicates three particular intervention areas: information, resources and logistics.

There needs to be a much wider dissemination of preparedness information and an integration of preparedness materials into daily life, college courses, high school curricula and text books. We make sure that our children know how to check for dangerous traffic—they need to be more informed about terrorism and have an embedded sense for planning. We also need a clear sense of what can and cannot be expected from government in case of need, so that there is a reasonable level of self-reliance. The resulting preparedness may eventually even become a competitive advantage.

Web-based training media should disseminate training. There should be co-opted media time to communicate terrorism-preparation activities. Why not think of video games and a TV soap opera dealing with preparedness for terrorism? After all, terrorism is global and its threat is more real than any reality show. Since many firms do not commit resources, and their shareholders do not support spending on terrorism-related tasks, an incentive needs to be provided. Support can either ease compliance with governmental rules or help firms pay for plans and preparations.

Security measures have introduced greater friction into international marketing that decreases the efficiency and effectiveness of logistics. Supply chain costs have increased substantially. Our survey respondents tell us that their international shipments now take an average of three days longer to arrive. Time is crucial when it comes to international competitiveness, merchandise shelf life, product quality and payment receipt. The new delays are evaluated to be the equivalent of a 2.4 percent tariff rate on goods, which is as large as the current overall level of protective tariffs imposed by Japan.

The gains from early preparation are high when compared with the costs. A capable response by firms to disaster is of benefit to the public purse. If public order and processes fall apart, the government will have to set things right at greater expense.

Firms that stay in business, retain their employees and serve their customers can make a great difference to societal continuity. As the saying goes—you can either pay now or pay later.

Are You Prepared for the New Surge of Countertrade?

International exchanges of goods and services are typically conducted with currencies, the value of which is settled by the four pillars of trust, demand, supply, and risk. If any of these pillars weaken, substitute exchange methods emerge, based on precious metals, commodities or even cigarettes. In light of economic and financial volatility in the U.S., Europe, and parts of Asia, we may again be heading for such substitutions in the global market.

Interest rates now underprice the true cost of capital. Global financial shifts around the world are frequent, easy, and large scale. Government debt repayment is uncertain. Currency blocs such as the euro are exposed

Originally published in the *Sri Lanka Guardian*, August 2, 2011. Used with permission of Michael R. Czinkota and the *Sri Lanka Guardian*.

to significant stress. The choice of the U.S. dollar as reserve a currency may be shifting. Financial debt and exposure are increasingly imbalanced.

As a result of all these instabilities, barter, buybacks, offsets and other forms of countertrade re-appear in the global market, offering new efficiencies in the conduct of trade. Companies need to understand how such international shifts will affect them, and learn to adjust their marketing and financing approaches to these new opportunities.

Countertrade is the use of goods, services, and other non-monetary resources as payment. Recent discussions with the Global Offset and Countertrade Association indicate that countertrade is on the rise due to government and company requirements.

Governments are concerned about the influence of large transactions on their country's balance of payments. They increasingly demand 'offsets' which are designed to reduce such influence. For example, in order to help pay for the acquisition of military airplanes, a country may demand that the seller of the planes encourages tourism to the country—as done by Egypt.

Concern is also growing about structural trade deficits. Governments and companies make countertrade a condition for importers. For example, Zaire and Italy exchanged scrap iron for 12 locomotives. China traded Russia 212 railway trucks full of mango juice in exchange for a passenger jet.

We like to think that only the free market sets prices. However, government influence and international necessity often build result in significant barriers to international exchanges. Countertrade agreements have shown that an exchange of goods for goods can overcome currency problems.

Historically, countertrade was used by soft currency countries, particularly in times of the Soviet Union. It has begun to rise again since the 2008–2009 financial crisis, bridging currency gaps and helping to reduce vast inventories. On a global scale, countertrade capability provides firms with a competitive edge. It keeps transactions alive and reduces the fear of high currency volatility. Many firms just want to carry on their business, rather than become currency speculators.

Companies know that an acceptance of non-cash payments can affect product values negatively. But as an alternative to no trade at all, countertrade looks better every day. Take the realities of a recent countertrade deal between Argentina and South Korea.

Argentina reported a trade deficit of $6 billion in 2010, driven in part by high automotive imports. With consumer demand for cars growing, Argentinean imports from Hyundai, the South Korean car company alone amounted to $91 million. Historically, the government handled such situations by simply restricting further imports. But international agreements and negotiations have sharply reduced this option.

The Financial Times reports that Hyundai distributors in Argentina utilized countertrade to compensate for the negative effects of car imports from Korea. They stimulated the sales of Argentinean agricultural goods, specifically peanuts, wine, and soy flour to South Korea.

Economic hardship is not the only incentive to countertrade. Bilateralism plays a large role in the acceptance of a countertrade offer. A country may encourage its companies to accede to barter requests from foreign trade partners and allies. The link between business and politics encourages such accommodation, even though doing so may be inconvenient. In the future, trading partners may reciprocate.

After decades of dormancy, countertrade is on track to again become a vital part of the global market. In a world of economic hardship, parsimony, and growing currency uncertainty, countertrade emerges as a viable solution for market and political shortcomings.

Companies are well advised to recast their strategy to reflect countertrade expectations and requirements. On the outreach side, new marketing and financing packages need to be prepared in order to remain ahead of the competition. Internally, personnel need to be hired and trained, to initiate such transactions, supervise them and see them through to long-term completion. Banks need to prepare for countertrade based financing and get ready to help clients use countertrade. In sum, we all need to get out of the focus of currency weaknesses and changes, and prepare for the resulting shifts in the conduct of international business.

Conviction, Vision led Reagan to Greatness

A great man has died, moving a piece of the present into history. It is a history that many of us have been part of and that shapes our future.

U.S. President Ronald Reagan's years in office were not easy. When a world power began living up to its billing, the domestic and international press labeled the Reagan administration as possessing only style over substance. Caricaturists loved to draw the president as a cowboy—with little knowledge or understanding of issues. Internationally, America was derided for having elected an "actor" as president. Domestically, the tax

Originally published in *The Japan Times*, June 12, 2004. Used with permission of Michael R. Czinkota and *The Japan Times*.

cuts were decried, as were the rising deficits, both of the budget and of trade.

Based on personal experience, I know that the president's alleged ignorance and detachment were not factual. While teaching international marketing at Georgetown University, I wrote frequent editorials for newspapers. One of them dealt with the demands by the U.S. auto industry to impose sharp limits on Japanese car imports. I wrote at the time that U.S. consumers chose those foreign cars primarily due to quality and price, and urged the president not to give in to protectionism but rather to exhort the Detroit producers to make better cars. Reagan read this editorial in his daily morning brief, and remarked that perhaps I could make a contribution to the administration. This man was not removed from the import of daily life—he did something about it!

When, after a requisite number of White House interviews, I joined the Commerce Department, I did so with a mission—to make government better, and to find ways to compete more effectively. It was a big step up from teaching that material in the classroom. The government colleagues I encountered were imbued with a similar spirit and were ready to work hard to achieve results. We were not an administration free of internal friction—far from it—but we never had to argue about which end of the rope we were pulling. We traveled like missionaries to bring the word to the world. The welcome mat was not even out with our close allies.

I recall visits abroad to discuss new elements of a tough export-control policy, of new steps toward privatization of traditional governmental activities, or the reinvigoration of a stalled round of trade negotiations. Our partners abroad expressed abhorrence at an overly demanding agenda, were repelled by our unrealistic expectations and were appalled by the prospect for change. I remember the derisive snorts we received from our friends with experience during the crises surrounding the stationing of missiles. I vividly recall the knowing eye rolls of the experts when Reagan urged Soviet President Mikhail Gorbachev to "tear down that wall."

We never listed the answers to give to unexpected questions. But we all knew what to do and what to say. We had a culture with an ingrained understanding of issues, instead of being run by a rulebook or bureaucratic controls.

Today we hear that Reagan was a great man—the global press and the many statements of condolences assure us that he was. But when did his many detractors decide that the transition to greatness occurred? Is it just because 15 years have passed since his term of office ended?

I believe it is because Reagan was a man of convictions and he had a vision of what he wanted to achieve. He followed through with single-mindedness, tolerating little if any distraction, because he understood how his success on the key issues would make a permanent difference in all of our lives. His commitment, dedication and willingness to set a direction resonated with all of us. He walked with kings but kept the common touch.

I have re-read Reagan's letter to me on January 19, 1989, his last full day in office. His words explain his thinking: "government has to work with us, not over us; to stand by our side not ride on our back; and you ensured that government remains the servant, not the master, of the hopes and dreams of our people." Thank you, President Reagan.

The European Prayer of Saint Augustine

The European Union grew from 15 to 25 members on May 1 2004. For 480 million Europeans, borders should have opened for free movement of people, ideas and commerce. But politics and politicians have sharply restrained that movement. Many in the old Europe fear disaster from a rapid influx of people. Workers from low-income nations within the expanded European Union (EU) could come to steal the few menial jobs still held precariously by locals. Immigrants may take advantage of generous health care, unemployment or welfare systems. And they'll never go home once they discover the burial benefits. The new EU members disagree. They point to a long history in which they have been occupied, exploited, and oppressed. Yet, they have never left their countries. Quite telling is the comment of a Hungarian who points out that "we live

With I. Ronkainen. Originally published in the *McDonough Business*, Spring/Summer 2004. Used with permission of Michael R. Czinkota and the *McDonough Business*.

in brick houses" to explain that families have stayed in place for centuries. Perhaps a few excursions abroad, but never a move!

Right now, fear has the political upper hand. The old European nations have implemented special escape clauses to safeguard their systems. An abundance of regulations are aimed against the new Europeans. For up to seven years, they will need special work permits, will be restricted in their unemployment and health care benefits, and constrained in their retirement programs. The current European expansion is remindful of the prayer of Saint Augustine: "Lord make me chaste—but not yet!" There are key drawbacks to such an arrangement. Delay introduces uncertainty, discontent and suffering. Those seeking benefits are disappointed. Their hopes of rapid improvement and dreams of equality are shattered. After a century of misery due to accidents of history and geography, here is another painful setback. It was, after all, EU proximity that enabled the new member countries to reform their economies and political systems in the short time period since the downfall of Communism.

Those seeking to postpone the effects of expansion only weaken their station. Jobs will continue to move to locations where they are performed better and at a lower price. There will be no inflow of new enthusiasm and elasticity. Rather than welcoming a shift to a new productive era, there is now a stultifying wait for the "inevitable," discouraging the old but not encouraging the new. Europe is different from the United States, but some post-World War II, U.S. experience can offer insights. Each year, on average, every seventh American moves. Most moves are within the same county, or within the same state. But year after year, U.S. movers to a different state almost reach three percent of the population. That is the equivalent of the entire U.S. population transitioning to a new home state in little more than one generation. Not everybody moves equally. The wealthy and well-entrenched have very low migration patterns. Those with low household incomes are the most avid movers, seeking new opportunities. Young adults move frequently to broaden their views. All this mobility has maintained a sense of adventure in America. It has retained a spirit of flexibility and exploration. If there are no new jobs in Illinois but lots of new opportunities in Arizona, then that's where many people go. There has been the creation of entirely new regional industry and service clusters, the absorption of many immigrants into the economy and relatively low long-term unemployment. There remains strong local pride of place yet there is little xenophobic fear from out-of-state migrants. Vermonters don't fear Virginians! What does all this mean for the new Europe? The opportunities to pick up and move are there, and those ready to move would fill a vital need. The decline in fertility and aging of the population will reduce the workforce by 5.5 percent by the year 2020 in the old EU. Even large increases in mobility would only represent a small population flow (which is now less than one half of one percent). People deserve to explore new options. New moves may well become an action signal for the European economy and way of thinking. This is a key opportunity to enrich the quality of life of regions and individuals. A long-term view is necessary. Migration may not result in permanent relocation. Individuals who go back home stimulate investment by setting up businesses and employing others. Many immigrants, rather than looking for a handout, want to develop their own base: home ownership, better educational opportunities, as well as health and economic security.

All these moves will change cultures. After all, culture is the result of learned behavior and adjustment to new conditions. Opening up to others should bring the reward of growing flexibility, better understanding, and rising tolerance levels. Mobility has brought the power of improvisation and adjustment to the United States. Today's world needs a Europe of courage, innovation and a willingness to take risks, with citizens that want new members to be part of, rather than apart, from them. It is time for traditionalists to discard the remaining barriers to mobility and to embrace with pride and happiness the new Europeans.

Farewell to Steve Jobs

We mourn the death of the premier international marketer of our century. We see his influence daily. We talk about consumer segments around the globe increasingly dancing together to the same music, and even singing the same tunes.

But how did they get to that level? iTunes made us become aware of each other's music, learning from each other, downloading the tunes to our iPods, so that we could dance. And now we can travel the world and achieve a very rapid and close understanding of the local music culture.

We also eat the same foods, sometimes with forks, but often also with chopsticks. Where did we learn that from? Remember, when computers

---

Originally published in *The Korea Times,* October 10, 2011, 1986. Used with permission of Michael R. Czinkota and *The Korea Times.*

were praised as a new tool to collect recipes? Seeing, preparing and sharing different kinds of foods were a clear outcome of Jobs' efforts.

We communicate with each other and are able to achieve overarching goals. For example, in recent times, many refer to the power of social media in bringing about political change. When we look at the "Arab Spring," much of it occurs because of the new links between people, the ability to organize and join forces.

In other words, these are iPhone moments. Steve Jobs has not made the world flat—he has interconnected it, and given us all a new spin and better mobility. For him, borders were no barriers, but merely points of information.

His work focused on and benefited the broad masses rather than the limited elites. He was a true spirit of and for the world. In practical terms, he has brought much freedom to the world.

Jobs has allowed smaller sized businesses to act like large ones; he has brought millions of new participants to the export table. His firm's work alone has had a dramatic impact on our balance of trade.

His innovations have transformed entire industries and made the world look toward the United States for innovation. He has enabled us all to obtain information which lets us react to changes and benefit from new opportunities.

He has made investments possible through the increasing ability to develop and understand data, and given us the tools to predict shifts and get ready for them. He made us dance, he brought us closer together. Some call him the Thomas Edison of our century. I think we should just call him Steve Jobs.

Farewell and thank you for all your work to strengthen people, and improve markets and lives.

Hungary's Economic Renewal

With the resurgence of nationalism in Eastern Europe, many post-communist liberation governments have been swept from power and replaced by reconditioned communists in socialist cloth.

That political shift might appear, at first glance, to presage a return to hard-line economic planning. But a recent visit to Hungary—one of the nations to make this political switch—provided persuasive evidence that market linking is taking hold and will not soon be displaced.

Originally published in the *Journal of Commerce*, December 12, 1996. Used with permission of Michael R. Czinkota and the *Journal of Commerce*.

Certainly, political pronouncements can give the wrong impression: Both public statements and policies are sometimes altered quickly and drastically. Moreover, there's some evidence that the post-communist era has brought some short-term profiteering; the presence of shining luxury cars is an indication.

Nevertheless, the behavior of most of the population shows how far market-oriented thinking has taken hold. Consider, for example, the state-owned Forum Hotel in Budapest. The room rates at this relatively modest establishment had risen to $300 a night—rather steep for Hungary.

However, right next door to the Forum is a new, privately owned Marriott Hotel. It had a special rate: $190 a night. I returned to the Forum Hotel and informed the desk clerk of my findings. In scarcely a blink, the price came down: The clerk offered a new rate—applied retroactively, no less—to $200 a night. Why $200 instead of $190? The difference would account for the luxury of staying without having to repack and move. Clearly, this clerk knew something about marketing.

A second experience a short while later confirmed the impression. I visited a pharmacy and asked for a particular brand of vitamins. The pharmacist inquired politely what problem I was trying to address. When told, he proceeded to explain that there was a better brand available at a very good price. In this case, too, marketing, as well as customer research and personal selling, were in evidence. The transformation of Hungary is far from complete, however. For some Hungarians, the societal changes have led to perverse conclusions.

During one lengthy dinner, for example, a government official argued vigorously in favor of state subsidies for authors of books on communist ideology. Those authors, he argued, can no longer draw a salary and therefore cannot sustain themselves on royalty income. Significantly, though, all the surrounding Hungarians vociferously disagreed.

There is, in Hungary, a sense that too much change has occurred too quickly, and that some of the changes have not been for the best. Large western-style food stores, for example, have taken over many Hungarian establishments. Rather than buy locally, these stores buy mainly from their customary western suppliers. As a result, fine Hungarian products have lost their local marketing outlets, not because of any fault in their products or pricing but because they are not part of the established supplier network.

Along with its economic transformation, Hungary is undergoing a reassessment of western values. This has been prompted by the gap between expectations of improvement under a market-oriented system and the actual improvement that has occurred so far. Among other things, Hungarians have discovered that western slogans and western products are not necessarily better than their domestic counterparts.

After four years of political and economic upheaval under communism, including squabbles within the government and high inflation, Hungarians are looking for a respite and some stability. All this will require some fresh perspectives and new approaches by western companies. It will no longer be enough for marketers to stress the western origin of goods. They must be able to form collaborative ventures with local partners. Those ventures that respond to the changing perspectives of Hungary's citizens will carry the day.

For example, marketers would do well to heed a growing sense of Hungarian pride in domestic manufactured goods, whether soft drinks, food, soap or even cellular telephones. The new, rapidly growing cellular telephone concern, Pannon, is a case in point; its name is derived from the old Latin word for Hungary, "Pannonia." Overall, Hungarians are becoming more sophisticated in the ways of the market. The curriculum at the Economics University and some of the other private Hungarian business schools, for example, is quite impressive.

More importantly, Hungarian ways of thinking, as well as work habits and attitudes toward the customer, show a rapid acceptance of a market-oriented approach. Perhaps the necessary catch-up time will turn out to be shorter than predicted. The political sentiment expressed in the elections does not seem to be a rejection of the market—just of politicians.

Making AID Work
in Russia

Foreign aid is a major target of Washington's budget cutters. Indeed, two goals tend to drive this discussion: cutting funding for Russia because some of its politicians are still communists, and cutting funding for the Agency for International Development because many of its activities are a waste.

When it comes to AID programs for Russia, then, Sen. Jesse Helms' colorful description—money poured down a rat hole—is a favorite of critics. In fact, the critics are wrong. Russia needs America's help, and AID is a good way to deliver it.

Originally published in the *Journal of Commerce,* November 27, 1995. Used with permission of Michael R. Czinkota and the *Journal of Commerce.*

Reforming and modernizing Russia's economic system will require enormous sums of money. Companies doing business there battle poor supply lines, non-existent distribution and service centers, limited rolling stock and inadequate transportation. Producers know little of quality control, inventory carrying costs, store assortment efficiencies and replenishment techniques—all basics of good business. Most Russian companies, in fact, barely understand the need for information exchange, integrated alliances between distributors and suppliers, and efficient communication systems, such as electronic data interchange. Yet each of these skills is crucial to developing Russia as a competitive economy.

In the case of the former East Germany, western Germany has transferred about $100 billion to rebuild the onetime communist state. Even so, the eastern economy has declined sharply and the people remain discontent. To match what East Germany received on a per capita basis, Russia would need more than $1 trillion in outside help. Russia, of course, has no such benefactor. It must attract money by creating trade and investment opportunities. The basis for this is a talented, capable work force. Building up this human capital will be essential to attracting financial capital.

The Agency for International Development can play an important role in developing Russia's human capital. Together with the telephone company U.S. West, AID funds the Center for Business Skills Development in Russia. Begun late last year, the center is well on its way to transforming the Russian business landscape.

Researchers at the center talked to Russians and found many who were anxious to learn western management and marketing techniques. With that in mind, the center is acquiring the best of western business knowledge and adapting it to the Russian environment, eliminating what doesn't fit and adding content that reflects Russia's unique needs.

With an emphasis on behavioral change, Russian students are taught decision-making, problem-solving, teamwork and profit orientation. Supervisors are trained in marketing, accounting and human resource management, while executives are exposed to strategic planning. Each course is critically evaluated, with a focus on how classroom learning can actually help individuals and their companies to perform better. All courses are translated and taught in Russian, and some focus on entry level employees.

So far progress is being made. Consider, for example, the Russian dispatcher who ran a car pool or taxi service. When a customer called for a car, the dispatcher typically would say he had none available, even though that was a lie. He would then wait a while and call the customer back, claiming he had just found a car. The point here was to convince the customer he had done him a great favor, thus building up good will that could be exchanged for something the dispatcher wanted.

This, of course, was the way business was done in the old Soviet Union: favors were traded because everything was in short supply and nothing worked well. The western business center taught the dispatcher that his job is to run an efficient car pool service, not play games with his customers. Today, when someone calls the dispatcher for a car, he gets it.

The U.S. business center also works with western and Russian institutions and firms. It collaborates with the World Trade Organization, Apple Computer and with Tekhnomash Rocket and Space Technology Co. After pretesting its courses with hundreds of students, the center's programs are becoming self-sustaining and are now offered throughout Russia. During the next few years, tens of thousands of Russians will be exposed to training sponsored by the center.

Because of the unique public/private nature of this venture, the cost per student for the U.S. government will be less than the price of a few textbooks. When the opportunity cost of not investing in the arms race is added in, this program produces a solid return on investment.

Indeed, the center represents the new AID. Its activities are effective, efficient and highly leveraged with private resources. Rather than working exclusively with governments, the center deals with people who are the seeds of social transformation. Its efforts are measured by results that can be observed and which are delivered quickly. And it addresses problems that are important to the United States and the world.

Yegor Gaidar, a former Russian prime minister, once said of his country's reforms, "Everything is reversible." That's probably an exaggeration, since democracy and the market seem to have taken root in Russia. Still, instability remains a threat, and it can be caused as much by poverty and unfulfilled expectations as by guns and tanks. Economic programs that draw people closer together build prosperity. AID's efforts in Russia make a difference, and they should be rewarded in the budget.

The Future of Trade in Developing Countries

In the growing world economy, the Northern Hemisphere can no longer rely solely on trade led by Fortune 500 corporations. Trade must also increase in the Southern Hemisphere for the benefits of globalization to continue.

Developing countries are strategically important to fostering an integrated global economic framework. Firms exporting to developing countries will expand into new markets, reaching consumers with increasing purchasing power. Firms importing from developing countries will gain access to high-quality, lower-cost products that improve their competitive edge.

With D. Belisle. Originally published in *The Journal of Commerce,* June 30, 1999. Used with permission of Michael R. Czinkota and *The Journal of Commerce.*

How is one to help developing countries while letting market forces prevail? Here we identify issues based on research conducted at Georgetown's McDonough School of Business. We then outline the market-oriented steps taken by the International Trade Center in Geneva. The key issues are globalization, new forms of partnership and information technology.

Concerning globalization: Worldwide manufacturing and sourcing strategies have made the production of goods cheaper, faster and better. To compete, producers must be able to measure their competitiveness and correct weaknesses. This requires market information, an ability to understand and forecast demand, and creative product adaptation and market niching.

These requirements are three strikes against developing countries: They have serious limitations in research and development, great difficulty in accessing trade information and often lack sophisticated marketing skills. Creativity and new technologies present these countries with opportunities for catching up with the industrialized world.

To become competitive, firms in developing countries must be able to measure and evaluate their performance. The International Trade Center has therefore developed a "competitiveness gauge" that enables firms to compare themselves with baseline data from manufacturers around the world. Producers anywhere can compare their production, organization and practices with those of enterprises in the same sector and know where to improve their performance. This tool also enables manufacturers to adapt their products to the quality expectations of their customers.

As for teamwork between government and business, it will become imperative as developing countries foray deeper into the global economy. Firms and governments must bury their mistrust and communicate constructively on strategies and collaboration. Firms also must share costs and lessons learned.

An emerging trend in the industrialized world is the sharing among firms of such assets as buildings, employees, telecommunications systems, transport facilities and the joint marketing of complementary products. Developing countries have to find their own models for such alliances.

The trade center has pioneered tools for exporters that address criteria for successful cooperation between the public and private sectors. These tools are kept 80 percent the same while 20 percent is customized to local needs. The Executive Forum on National Export Strategies scheduled by the trade center scheduled regularly will review the success of partnership-based export-development strategies.

In information technology, lack of a telecommunications infrastructure is no longer a handicap. The investment required to establish a basic national telecommunications system has fallen drastically, allowing private firms to bring telecommunications to a country within two years. The question therefore is not if, but when, developing countries will participate in e-commerce.

The International Trade Center serves as these countries' one-stop shop for guidance on implementing e-commerce strategies. It trains government officials, firms and trade support institutions. It advises on cyber marketing, international purchasing, and the legal, financial, quality and logistical aspects of e-commerce for manufactured goods as well as services.

Responding to needs identified through research, the trade center offers programs matching exporters with importers, profiles port strategies for services, sponsors online exhibitions of products from developing countries, and answers the most frequently asked questions on e-commerce.

The implementation of the World Trade Organization multilateral agreements has brought about unprecedented growth in international trade. Helping developing countries to capitalize on it is essential. They must be assisted in practical ways to catch up with the industrialized world.

Trade with firms in these countries will lower production costs and the costs of importing and expand market access. Without the support of trade, the chances for continued development and stability will be in jeopardy for both the Northern and Southern hemispheres.

Open Ivory Tower Windows for Fresh Air

Universities are among the most successful institutions that mankind has created in the last millennium. But what role do universities need to play in the knowledge society of tomorrow to continue their success story?

This question grows more pressing for the western welfare states, as their dominance in research and innovation is being challenged by globalization and the dynamics of the emerging economies.

The example of the United States, which like no other nation has been able to benefit from universities as drivers of growth, makes this abundantly clear. For a long time America has combined cutting-edge

---

With A. Pinkwart. Originally published in *The Korea Times*, July 12, 2011. Used with permission of Michael R. Czinkota and *The Korea Times*.

research not only with strong science and engineering but also with entrepreneurially oriented business schools. With this approach the country has promoted groundbreaking innovations.

Yet, since the bursting of the Internet bubble, there are increasing doubts as to whether the previous innovation concepts still fit the new and future challenges and research priorities.

The advancement of biotechnology and social sciences absorbs almost half the research funds of U.S. universities. Add the expansion of national security and military research, and universities have lost important drivers for the industrial use of new scientific insights.

Instead, the ivory towers, which were believed to be abandoned, have returned. Like the hanging sword of Damocles the gigantic budget deficit will also require new structures and processes in research and teaching at universities.

Germany may currently look better with its broad mix of industrial and service-related innovations and its strong and flexible small and medium-size businesses.

However, this should not obscure obvious weaknesses. What has been achieved with the excellence and high-tech initiatives and more autonomy for universities in recent years is threatened to be lost again with ideologically-motivated campaigns against an alleged commoditization of higher education.

Germany and the United States are facing similar problems. So far the American and the German university systems have learned from each other in a time delayed fashion. Now, due to mounting competitive and financial pressures, universities need to learn simultaneously from each other.

The transatlantic exchange of ideas at a conference in Washington a few days ago made it very clear: University success is not about tearing down the ivory towers, but to open their windows as far as possible to other disciplines and to new markets. While the freedom of teaching and research have to be defended, at the same time strong bridges for mutual transfers have to be built.

In the 19th century, Alexander von Humboldt revamped the western education system by insisting on the scientific approach to research. We now need a set of Humboldt kind of ideas for the 21st century.

The university of the future is only viable if best research and best teaching go hand in hand with best knowledge transfers. To achieve these goals, universities need reliable funding and high productivity. Interdisciplinary linkages, a close integration with the ecosystem as well as research excellence and relevance are also necessary. All this calls for major cultural change on both sides of the Atlantic. For a faster industrial use of new scientific knowledge both in universities and in businesses one has to rethink current approaches. We need more risk capital, new business models, and efficient intermediary organizations in order to build a sturdy bridge over the wide valley of death between basic research and innovation.

The efforts are worthwhile. Key is not just wealth and employment; it is all about the development opportunities of each individual and the defense of our freedoms. These provide the ideas and energy for the design of the next stage of our universities and our societies.

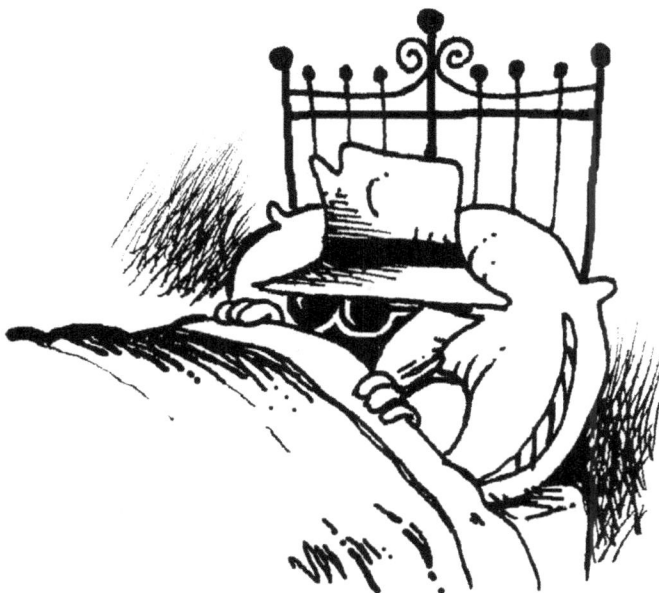

Is it Just Me?

Going for the new and unknown is my job. I am a university professor and do my professing through research, teaching, and writing. Most of my activities tend to be new.

I never really know how a class discussion will turn out. When formulating research hypothesis the whole idea is to be wide open to new indications and findings. And even in the 10th edition of my textbook, there are major new directions and changes to be captured.

Yet, thinking new or unexpected thoughts is disquieting to some. For example, I still dream of living some day in a castle. To many friends and neighbors, this is one of those silly dreams which should have been shed decades ago.

Originally published in *The Korea Times*, October 10, 2011. Used with permission of Michael R. Czinkota and *The Korea Times*.

Sometimes, when I describe my castle, people even get openly hostile, declaring such thoughts to be outlandish, wasteful and reflective of delusions of grandeur. They tell me that spending even a minute on such ideas takes away from productivity and is a giant waste.

But I've discovered that I may not be alone. On occasions when I mention castles, I see eyes light up, reflecting dreams remembered and imagination recaptured. The voices might be slightly lowered, but the intensity of the conversation picks up.

Sometimes we even repair to the Internet and do some searches. Entering, for example, "Schloss Verkauf" under Google brings up the hunting castle in Magdeburg, the castle with the moat near Berlin, the family castle from the 16th century in Bavaria. There are many more in Austria, Switzerland, France, and Italy.

Some of them come with an ante-castle area of large proportion. Many have the requisite tower, the horse stables and the huge gate. Then there are those with bordering forest areas or vineyards.

Some are fully restored, others need some help, but they all require loving tender care—if only because preservation regulations require it. The price typically seems reasonable or even low when compared with real estate prices in many of the metropolis.

I am told about the deleterious effects of a castle. There are the terrible tax burdens, the upkeep and maintenance nightmares, the isolation, and the total excess of space.

Forests may mean that one has to pay for a forester. Woods will have to be scouted regularly for infested trees. The deer population will have to be managed. Who shovels the snow in winter? All, so true.

But then I think of my youth, when dreaming about special things was not out of reach, but rather part and parcel of life. Over time, not too many dreams of childhood have been preserved.

Yet, the move to a castle is not an introverted return to the olden days, but in its own way a new, pioneering action. A new environment, an entirely different set of challenges, new neighbors, combined with history and closeness to nature.

It's also a new perspective. Castles, by their very nature, tend to have a far-reaching outlook. Typically they are built on top of a hill or even a mountain, with the tower reaching well above the trees. After all, you want to see who is coming up the road.

Just as the climbing of a mountain lets you see vistas never taken in before, a castle gives an overview. A castle reflects promises of safety and freedom. There is an aura of peace and a welcoming of guests. A certain ampleness is also built into castles. There is the knights room, the salon, the dining hall, and of course, the ballroom. What a feeling of open space!

As time flies by, in many societies one is encouraged to settle down, which means to settle for what we have. Contentment eliminates pain. But it also pours concrete onto our limitations and focuses us on the low end of the horizon. By contrast, sleep research tells us that dreams help sustain life. Perhaps even God was dreaming when he did his creating.

Castles are not easy. Even the Bavarian King Ludwig, who built Neuschwanstein, the model for later replicas by Disney, learned that harsh reality. When he built too many castles, he was deposed, and, some say murdered. I think that we all need our castles.

We're all born with some, we drop them often, but there is a time to have our dreams return. A castle can be our defiance of time, our dedication to life and culture. You don't have to be a king to dream, but if you get your castle, you will be a king.

Terrorism and International Business

The airplanes of 9/11 forced countless multinational corporations (MNCs) to update their strategic planning. Our work with executives at more than 150 MNCs shows that 10 years later, companies are still grappling with how best to manage the terrorist threat.

In the two decades before 2001, the rate at which firms launched international ventures was growing rapidly. After 9/11, foreign direct investment fell dramatically as firms withdrew to their home markets. The popularity of international-sounding company and brand names decreased appreciably as managers now emphasize domestic and local affiliations.

The tendency to reverse course on globalization has been accompanied by declining international education in the United States, as revealed

With G. Knight and G. Suder. Originally published in the *Korea Times*, September 4, 2011. Used with permission of Michael R. Czinkota and the *Korea Times*.

by falling enrollments in foreign language and international business courses. In the past decade, managers shifted much of their focus from proactive exploration of international opportunities to a defensive posture emphasizing threats and vulnerable foreign operations.

In Europe, the radicalization of individuals and groups, motivated by ideology, religion or economic concerns, threatens local cooperation and social harmony. European business schools have benefited from tighter restrictions on international student enrollments in the U.S., but the focus of teaching has shifted from global to regional trade.

Another outcome of the terrorism threats has been a rise of public-private partnerships, in which governments and firms collaborate to counter them. For example, global police agencies now partner regularly with private firms to combat cyber crime and attacks on critical computer infrastructure.

Governments and activist groups now use social media to organize campaigns fighting against threats ranging from dictators to disease. But nations also have begun to curtail social media when they are contrary to government interests.

The cost of protecting against terrorism is many billions, while terrorist spend millions or less on their actions. There are abundant opportunities for small groups to employ non-weapon technologies, such as aircraft, to cause massive harm.

Though our capacity to protect key facilities has improved over time, the security focus on high-value assets encourages terrorists to redirect their violence at "soft targets" such as transportation systems and business facilities. Greater security at home means attacks will increasingly take aim on firms' foreign operations.

Companies have placed more emphasis on terrorism risk considerations when choosing how to enter foreign markets. In the last century, foreign direct investment (FDI) was the preferred approach. But terrorism has shifted the balance.

Now many more firms favor entry through exporting, which permits broad and rapid coverage of world markets, reduces dependence on highly visible physical facilities, and offers much flexibility for making rapid adjustments.

In terms of economies of scale and transaction costs, FDI is generally superior, but the risks of exporting are judged to be lower. Markets tend to punish failure more harshly than they reward success, which makes risk-minimizing strategies more effective.

Skillful management of global logistics and supply chains cuts the risk and cost of downtime. Firms seek closer relations with suppliers and clients in order to develop more trust and commitment. Some have increased "on-shoring" by bringing suppliers back into the country when their remoteness constitutes risk.

Terrorism causes an organizational crisis whose ultimate effects may be unknown, and poses a significant threat to the performance of the firm. Corporate preparedness for the unexpected is a vital task. Innovative managers develop back-up resources, and plan for dislocations and sudden shocks with a flexible corporate response.

Terrorism is a public threat, and some managers believe government should bear the cost of protecting against it. Others argue that a public-private partnership is the most effective approach, with firms taking the lead.

There is also the issue whether corporate headquarters or the locally exposed subsidiary should fund prevention and preparation expenditures. Regardless of who pays, everyone can agree on the need to guard against terrorism.

Every world region is vulnerable, and most attacks are directed at businesses and business-related infrastructure. Terrorism requires decision-making and behaviors that support vigilance and development of appropriate strategies. Managers who fail to prepare run the risk of weaker performance or even loss of the firm.

While we can no longer choose the lowest cost option, 10 years after 9/11 companies are more aware, less exposed, and less vulnerable to the risk of terrorism. But in the next 10 years comes the really big task: What can and should we do collectively and individually to reduce the causes of terrorism.

Business Can Make
a Difference

The "War on Terror" was launched 10 years ago, on October 7, 2001. It represents a battle against terrorism, extremism and global geopolitical adversity seen to oppose democracy and freedom of choice.

In the intervening years, however, the war has produced various unintended consequences that threaten personal freedom and other liberties enjoyed by progressive societies worldwide.

With G. Knight and G. Suder. Originally published in the *Korea Times*, October 4, 2011. Used with permission of Michael R. Czinkota and the *Korea Times*.

Stringent inspections delay cargo and personnel at border crossings. In many cities, cameras constantly monitor the movement of vehicles and civilians alike.

Government wiretapping and surveillance procedures have been expanded. Bank transactions are scrutinized as never before. Airport security measures are annoying and sometimes even humiliating. In many ways, such intrusions represent a victory for terrorists.

An early casualty of the War on Terror was Afghanistan. During much of the time since October 2001, Afghans have seen little improvement in their lives and business conditions.

Ten years on, Foreign Policy labels Afghanistan a "failed state," especially regarding security, refugees, and legitimacy of the state. As the United States prepares an acceptable exit strategy, Afghanistan faces much risk and uncertainty.

Divided by religious and political strife, the country's per-capita income remains among the lowest worldwide. Adult literacy is below 28 percent and infant mortality is high. Following 30 years of war, Afghanistan's social, institutional, and commercial infrastructures are in a decrepit state.

The World Bank and World Trade Organization (WTO) have pointed to constraints that discourage corporate investment in Afghanistan: crime and disorder, inadequate energy and transport systems, and insufficient access to finance.

However, experts also suggest that, with appropriate local knowledge and collaborative efforts, companies can succeed in Afghanistan.

Success requires investments in education and training, creation of networks and infrastructure, and open-mindedness and flexibility toward the unexpected. Firms with significant experience in troubled regions are most likely to succeed.

Recent changes in Afghanistan have produced significant potential opportunities for early investors, especially in infrastructure development. The World Bank views Afghanistan as a prospective hub for regional trade.

The WTO points to significant improvements in the categories of "getting credit" and "registering property." Thanks to a modern secured transactions law that helps companies obtain loans, Afghanistan is now well ranked for "starting a business."

Afghanistan's economy is improving, especially in agriculture, commodities, and traditional industries. The nation is home to a wealth of natural resources, including natural gas, petroleum, and certain key minerals. It has benefited from billions of dollars of international aid and investments. In many ways, Afghanistan is typical of troubled regions around the world.

Experience with Afghanistan and the War on Terror has provided important lessons for western governments and businesses alike. Companies now include terrorism as an important factor in their international planning.

Firms are devising international strategies that emphasize flexibility and the ability to change course quickly, with less dependence on vulnerable physical facilities.

Foresight and skillful management reduce the risk of loss and downtime. Companies are putting more emphasis on developing closer relations with governments and other key players in uncertain foreign markets.

Since the launch of the War on Terror, many world regions have experienced attacks and conflict. But companies are fighting back. Experienced managers are vigilant and favor approaches that ensure long-term, sustainable success.

Simultaneously, governments are learning to strike the right balance between security and unneeded intrusions in business and our personal lives.

Educators like us have an important role to play. Alongside managers and public authorities, we share a responsibility to redefine global commerce.

Increasingly, business must emphasize attitudes and behaviors that are not just ethical, but also socially responsible, compassionate, and focused on the long-term stability of nations worldwide.

Perhaps the best hope for a brighter future in troubled regions is business that, in addition to expanding profits, meets the social and economic needs of local stakeholders.

The struggle against terror, extremism and adversity is a long-term effort. The costs in human and financial terms are extremely important.

But hope remains eternal. Responsible, collaborative business can go far toward improving the social, political and economic landscape worldwide.

The global business community has both the capacity and responsibility to protect against the terrorist threat and to support development of a more sustainable, peaceful world.

The Cartagena Incident: Affirming U.S. Success

During the past days emotions have been running high about the U.S. Secret Service dalliance with ladies of the night in Colombia. An 'incident' has mushroomed into a self-inflicted 'policy debacle.' Some policy makers, in describing this apparent scurge of mankind, appeared to recommend firing everyone who ever had lust in their hearts. The Senate majority leader's solution is to hire many more women for the Service. Others suggest that protocols and training for protective details need

With I. Leoncio. Originally published in *Ovi Magazine*, May 8, 2012. Used with permission of Michael R. Czinkota and *Ovi Magazine*.

to be tightened; even the possible use of the 'honey trap' strategy is suggested by some. A merchant seaman with great experience writes in an editorial that the lesson learned should be to 'always pay your bill'! President Obama, who was the object of all the protection, used the annual White House correspondents dinner to crack jokes about the affair. I find all the public anxiety vastly misplaced, and the event's effect on the U.S. reputation misinterpreted.

Most of what has been reported portrays the affair as a letdown by and of the United States. Since fraternizing with female escorts violates the self-image of puritanism, weakens the state of bliss in a marriage, and possibly may distract officers from their duties the next day, the transgression of the Secret Service has been labeled as evil incarnate. However, there are not just vile aspects to the apparently unheard of one night stands. It is very important to interpret such occurrences as to their meaning in a local and global context. Experiences with night workers are not necessarily bad or useless. Here is a personal example which one of us wrote about in 1990:

"On a visit through various of the newly emerging democracies, I noticed never before encountered quantities of ladies of the night in hotel lobbies and restaurants. The fact that I was easily identified as a Western visitor appeared to contribute markedly to my attractiveness. The result were various conversations, a typical one of which is presented here:

(O)ldest (P)rofession: You American?

R(otund) T(ourist): Yes

OP: Interested? One thousand dollars.

RT: Isn't that a bit much? How much do you earn on your
        daytime job?

OP: I am a secretary and make $40 a month. Here my price is
        $1,000. Americans can afford it.

RT: Have you done any business yet?

OP: Not so far, but some day I will.

RT: What if I ask any of the other ladies?

OP: They also charge a thousand dollars. We have talked, and we
        are now a free market. But you have to stay with me. I talked
        to you first."

There was much reflection of society in these conversations. First, there was the desire to become a private entrepreneur. With restrictions removed, the opportunity beckoned. Initiative, if left un-channeled, may, however, lead to unexpected and sometimes undesirable market manifestations. Second, the idea of profit was at the forefront of the mind. While the meaning of profit and the understanding of profitability can differ widely, it's about the money! Reneging on a transaction is a betrayal of trust. Competition may be seen differently, as may market power, but it is a hard lot to have to knuckle under to others with power. Finally, relationships and expected outcomes must be seen in the context of both sides.

Here is why I consider the Cartagena incident a feather in the cap of the United States. It is no mean feat for a small country like Colombia, or for a new ladies of the night to complain against the representatives of the most powerful nation in the world ... and to prevail. This is a triumph for the U.S. after decades of trying to endow others with equal rights and of proselytizing that any misconduct (even down to paying a bill) be addressed fairly and openly. The inability of U.S. Secret Service personnel to dictate terms was a breakthrough.

How does this compare historically when Rome's pro-consuls served in the provinces, when Genghis Khan's hordes swamped the steppe, when the Ottoman soldiers entered Constantinople? There may have been complaints and unhappiness on part of the locals, but there was no report, no reparation, and certainly no punishment of the troops.

The United States has brought new empowerment to nations around the globe. If one looks at one century of U.S. influence on the world, and asks: are countries better off? the answer must be yes. America has strengthened the power of the individual, the ability to state one's case, to be heard, and to receive a remedy for injustice. In our research at Georgetown University's business school, we call this 'curative business' where old unfairness and inequality gets fixed. What a glorious achievement!

Greeks must be proud every time their standard bearer leads all the other flag carriers into the Olympic stadium in commemoration of Greece having brought the games to the world. So will the U.S. be perennially proud for having propelled mankind up to the plateau of self determination, actualization, assortment, and the pursuit of happiness. Now that's much more important than the personal failures of a few men.

Index

businessexpert
Press

Be Sure To Check Out Czinkota's First Book
With This Same Terrific Flair . . .

*As I Was Saying . . . Observations on
International Business and Trade Policy,
Exports, Education, and the Future*

www.businessexpertpress.com